IMPROV AT WORK

WHAT THE BUSINESS WORLD CAN LEARN FROM IMPROVISATIONAL COMEDY

NICOLE FAUST COHEN

IMPROV AT WORK

What the Business World Can Learn from Improvisational Comedy

By
Nicole Faust Cohen

Improv at Work:
What the Business World Can Learn from Improvisational Comedy
Published by Elite Online Publishing
63 East 11400 South
Suite #230
Sandy, UT 84070

COHEN, FAUST, NICOLE, Author
IMPROV AT WORK
NICOLE FAUST COHEN

ISBN: 978-1-956642-05-6 (Paperback)
ISBN: 978-1-956642-04-9 (eBook)

BUS030000
HUM010000

Editing: Eileen Ansel Conery

QUANTITY PURCHASES: Companies, universities, professional groups, clubs, and other organizations may qualify for special terms when ordering quantities of this title. For information, email info@eliteonlinepublishing.com.

To my husband, Mike, and our kids, Zach and Sabrina.
Three of my very favorite humans.
You make me better each day.

In honor and memory of my dad, Stanley Faust.

Table of Contents

PREFACE

We have the power to change the workplace. It's ours after all. We spend so much time working. For most of us, we spend our entire adult lives working. Let's make it better. More human, more meaningful. Better.

Now more than ever the business world needs an inspirational guide aimed at transforming today's stressed, rushed, and struggling work environment into a more upbeat, collaborative, and creative environment, similar to the one surrounding the improvisational comedy "improv" world. *Improv at Work* is a guide that explores the profound impact that improv can have on the business world from the perspective of someone who has both business and improv experience.

We are heading into a time when we should see the most incredible levels of innovation possible on our planet. Our global community is connected wirelessly in a way that never existed before in history. Tasks that used to fill our days, like walking around in a grocery store or managing financials in a physical bank, are disappearing, freeing our minds to focus on higher-level activities. And technology will continue to make life easier. However, with all these advancements, we are interacting with each other face-to-face much less.

Innovation emerges when teams collaborate effectively and creatively to produce something new. The best collaborators use communication that is clear and thoughtful. Good communication is strongest when human interactions are optimized, enabling all parties to express themselves confidently and openly.

If we want to realize the full potential of what's possible in the workplace, we must avoid neglecting our own interpersonal skill development.

We will find it difficult to grow as innovators with strong human interaction skills when we continue to substitute the majority of human conversations with devices and emojis. Few business ideas and industry solutions are brainstormed, collaborated upon, and further negotiated into new businesses and new agreements over texts.

This is where improv fits into the picture.

From the vantage point of one of the working world's own, I'll dive into insights on why the business world needs better innovation, collaboration, communication, and human interaction now more than ever. Improvisational comedy is a practice requiring the same. I'll compare business and improv based on the need and examples in both worlds. For example, both worlds require creativity, empathy, teaming, confidence, strong listening skills, defined outcomes, and the list goes on and on.

Later, we'll review a set of seven improv rules that should and can be applied to the business world. Each rule has its own chapter where we'll explore the rule and acknowledge why it is relevant to business and to improv and how that rule has been respected, or more common than not, broken in business. Just as actors must learn the rules by performing, we'll explore how to bring the rules to life at work with easy-to-follow activities and games, which have been tested successfully in business workshops with high-performing leadership teams. We'll then review a set of both considerations and warnings as further take-aways as you explore the rule and the activities on your own.

Finally, we'll close with suggested action plans for individuals and teams to bring these activities into practice in the short- and longer-terms.

This book is intended for professionals to keep handy and use repeatedly — they'll want to play the activities with colleagues and bring those activities home to practice with family and friends.

Consider this a resource to drive teams on a better path towards the workforce we all desire: outcomes driven, inspiring, and fun.

No costumes required. Let's get started.

I

HUMAN INTERACTION AT A CROSSROADS

Back in the day

For generations, humans were forced to interact without agendas. We didn't schedule discussions every time we wanted to connect. Sentences weren't made up of just acronyms and emoticons. We talked in the moment, and we did that a lot.

And we loved it. We learned from it. We learned from one another. We improved our interactions.

Back in the day — okay, maybe not so long ago — we blissfully went about our day, exchanging words without knowing where the conversation would go, without knowing how long it would last. And that was okay. That unknown was acceptable. Even fun for many.

I had many different personal experiences with these types of unplanned interactions growing up in Cincinnati, Ohio — on the phone, down the street, and just about anywhere.

First, the phone interaction. I used to welcome any interruption of play when the home phone line rang. It meant there would be a race to the landline with a cord that only got stretched longer the more we fought over it. Sometimes multiple family members would answer the line — "I got it," "No, I got it," "It's probably for me," or "Hang up already!" Without knowing who was on the other line, I'd answer the phone eagerly, "Hello?" At times I might mix it up with a "Hello… Faust residence." With that opening out of the way, I waited for the person calling to reveal who was on the other line. I was only seconds away from potentially talking with a school mate or my dad's third cousin. It could be my mom's friend, Shelley, and I would have to suffer through a few minutes of awkward dialogue.

"How's school going?"
"Fine."
"What's your favorite subject this year?"
"All of them."
"Are you going anywhere for break?"
"I don't know."

It seemed like forever, but eventually she would ask, "Is your mom there?" To which I would quickly reply, "Yes, I'll get her." I had to put the phone down since it was, after all, attached to the wall, and run all over the house to find my mom.

Second, down the street interaction. Then there was my middle school Saturday morning routine of springing out of the house, darting down the street, and walking up a friend's driveway to ring a doorbell and ask, "Is Sarah home?" Of course, she was home — it was Saturday morning, she was 12 years old, and there were cartoons to watch and a video game to play. Nonetheless, I would ask the question politely to her mom, who would then scream up the stairs for Sarah to come down. This was followed by a few minutes of conversation. Though those few minutes may have felt awkward to me having to speak to a grown-up, it was time spent practicing the art of interacting with another human.

"How are you?"

"Fine."

"How's your mom?"

"Good."

"Are you excited about next week's field trip?"

"I don't know, I think so."

> *Wow, that was a lot of words exchanged with an adult on a Saturday morning, I would think, but never say aloud.*

Regardless of the exact amount of time it took my friend to make her way to the doorway, I was unknowingly getting good practice interacting with the universe. Face-to-face. Eye contact. Unplanned. In the moment. Eventually, with this type of interaction over years, I would learn to give more descriptive answers, and ask questions back, smile, and engage in a more authentic way without an expression of agony.

Third, anywhere interactions. Awkward, unplanned, and uncomfortable exchanges were everywhere those days. Anyone remember frequently going into the bank to talk with an actual person? I do. I would walk into the bank and talk to the bank teller, a real human. If I was with my mom, usually the conversation was very similar to the one with my mom's friend, Shelley. But this time it was in person so I could at least entertain myself by staring at lipstick on the teeth while the teller handed me a bank calendar for the third time that month and told me about the importance of saving money. Sometimes I even got a quarter.

> *No judgment on the lipstick on the teeth part; most of us know, lipstick is complicated. How can we expect it not to get a little messy?*

Waiting in lines, for a service or a product. No fast tracking. No ordering ahead of time to walk in and quickly grab a drink and bag of food. I had to *actually talk* to the people in line around me. Conversations started up as easily as a comment on the weather, "I heard it's supposed to be rainy all weekend" or as easily as a comment on the line itself, "I don't think we have moved at all in 30 minutes." Engagement was easy then, because quite honestly, there was nothing else to do while waiting in line. Stare off into the distance? Focus on breathing? I would make the most out of standing next to another human being and chat them up. It seemed to make the time pass with greater tolerability.

Now wouldn't it have been great if I could have closed this topic by sharing that I in fact met the love of my life while standing in line? Yes, that would have been fun. A cute story about how we met, started up a conversation while waiting in line at the local bank. We joked about savings bonds, oh how we laughed! A nice story, making the point about the power of striking up conversations, engaging with humans. Of course, it would have been a fictional story, but a cute story, nonetheless.

Back to the walk through memory lane...

Years ago, if food was going to make its way from a restaurant to our home, it absolutely would require human interaction. I actually had to have a conversation on the phone with someone to order the food, and most likely, hand payment to a real person when the food arrived at the door. As social as I thought I was, I definitely was not the person in my family who ever wanted to answer the door and talk to the person coming to our house. I know, surprising, especially given what I shared about my reaction when the phone rang *"I'll get it!"* In this case, I would run in the opposite direction when a real person, whom we did not know by the way, walked up to our door. Eventually though, after being kindly asked to answer it, "You wanted the pizza, get the door," I was subject to the exchange of words at the front door, though minimal, and received yet even more practice on speaking with humans unscripted.

How did we find out which plumber to use, which TV to buy, or at which hotel to stay? That's right, we talked to people. Those people could be the ones standing next to us in a line somewhere or just those in our community. Regardless, recommendations were requested and received in person. What we then did with that recommendation was up to us, of course. I always smiled when my dad asked a restaurant staff member for recommendations on entrées. Not sure how he could trust someone he just met for something as important as our meal. What if that particular person gave horrible advice just for fun? What if he ate ketchup on green beans? We trusted this complete stranger to provide the best entrée selection! Regardless, conversation emerged. Thoughts were exchanged. My dad had to think on his feet to engage this person in a meaningful conversation in the moment, as I watched and learned.

> *My apologies if this reference offended you if you do in fact eat ketchup with your green beans. We are each entitled to make unique food choices.*

People in social, non-professional settings had to interact *a lot*. And it was in those social ad hoc interactions where the practice happened. It was this practice to refine our human interaction skills that would become necessary later in life to drive successful outcomes and business results. People had to talk to people: parents' friends, random callers, friends' parents, fellow concertgoers, food delivery professionals, and your own family and friends.

Back then those of us in the workforce talked to people in real time and without hesitation. If we were lucky enough to have an office, we went into the office and started to work. If we had a question or thought it best to collaborate with a colleague, we got up, and walked over to that person to ask that question or to think through a problem. We talked with one another until the conversation came to a natural close, and we typically felt pretty good about that interaction. When we went into a break room, we chatted with people we knew, as well as people we didn't know. When we had a funny story to share, we shared it. Right there and then. With real people in front of us. They laughed, or not, but either way we instantly knew if they liked what we shared, didn't get it, or thought we were idiots. We then modified the content or delivery for next time. We improved each time.

As painful as some of those conversations could be, while others were far more fun, what was improving? We were getting better every day — at talking, listening, accepting conversation pauses, and just being ourselves. In each of those moments, we learned how to be comfortable without knowing exactly with whom we would interact and without knowing exactly what we were going to say. We were open to the mystery and possibilities of in-person interaction.

Today

Many things are different now and so much is better. We have the ability to talk to anyone, at any time, and without long distance charges. We can share a thought immediately digitally through our fingertips. If anything happens anywhere, we get "breaking news" alerts on our phones, watches, eyeglasses, and perhaps soon, even earrings.

We no longer run to pick up the home phone if it's not for us, if we don't know the person, if we don't want to — or just because plenty of us don't have a home phone anymore or use it at all. According to the National Center for Health Statistics, in 2003, nearly 95 percent of adults had a landline. In 2021, that number decreased to less than 40 percent.

What that means for many of us landline-less is that we're wireless. When we answer a call, that call is intended for us with a device that fits in our handbag or in our pocket.

We don't typically answer someone else's cell phone and engage in the kind of random phone call from years ago. Today, if my mom's friend Shelley is calling, it will be a call directly to my mom's cell phone, and it would be my mom, and *only* my mom, who would answer that call.

Going to the bank and starting up conversations? How yesteryear. Most of us don't go into a bank on a regular basis. We might visit the bank on the occasional activity that requires some assistance, but it's rare, very rare for most of us to frequent the bank's physical spaces with so many contactless banking options available to us.

Who still strikes up a conversation in line? I have few friends who still do this, but most often: who has time to strike up a conversation when our faces are intimately engaging with a mobile device, smart phone, digital game, social app, news feed, or weather update? Why ask a stranger to comment on whether or not it will be rainy on Saturday when about 100 apps can give us the same information and with greater accuracy?

Let's talk about ordering food. Calling in a food order? Talk to a real person? We don't need to talk to anyone if we don't want to. Now we can order our food online and pay for it online. If we do pick up our food, we can pick it up from a restaurant on a countertop, avoiding an interaction altogether. If the food does come to our homes, most delivery services leave the food on the doorstep like it's a daily newspaper. So, we can open the door, take the bag, and then shut the door without talking to anyone.

Since we don't need to ask a live person for recommendations anymore, we can avoid even more people in a conversation. Plenty of websites and phone apps will tell us more than we need to know regarding any kind of service or purchase we're considering. We don't need to rely on anyone to give us an entrée recommendation. Instead, we can rely on "group think" and make an informed selection based on 37 reviews; undoubtedly there are 37 people just like us, so surely those recommendations are trustworthy and will lead us to a successful outcome. Surely.

Kids no longer need to ask a librarian how to find the capital of a country or learn whether an animal is a carnivore or nocturnal. Kids don't need to talk to anyone to find anything. We can, like hermit crabs, sit in our shells and learn what we need to learn all by ourselves with the use of our friendly World Wide Web.

At work, people schedule time to talk to someone else if they can get on calendars. Questions are typically conveyed over email or instant chatting. When we have something funny to share, we share it electronically and wait for digital thumbs up counts to determine how we feel about ourselves for the rest of the day. Sherry didn't comment or like it? She's dead to me. Adjust how we deliver our funny remarks to friends? Sure, Twitter to Facebook. LinkedIn to Instagram. Got it covered. All from within our secure shells.

But can we optimally learn what we really need to learn in order to be successful in the world and inspire each other out of the comfort of our own shell? Protected from spontaneous conversations? Locked into our comfort zones?

II

BUSINESS WORLD UNDER CRISIS

Without the interaction practice and barrier-free conversation in personal and professional interactions, what is obviously lost becomes quite evident in the business world.

This loss manifests itself in our inability to communicate and collaborate, ideate and create with each other at our best, as well as our inability to build the kinds of relationships that grow through the thoughtful exchange of words, thoughts, facial expressions, and stories. Our exchanges have become compartmentalized, time-boxed, and overly processed. Less unscheduled and spontaneous. We're growing less confident in our ability to navigate through unchartered waters of conversation.

Workplaces around the world are complex and are fostering environments where it is becoming increasingly difficult to build the interaction skills necessary for optimal communication, collaboration, and innovation, three of the most critical expectations of high-performing and thriving businesses. We all know this is true, but let's look at some specific reasons explaining why.

1. Entering the Workplace with Less Human Interaction

Generations entering or new to the workplace are doing so having grown up surrounded by less and less human interaction.

The generations of talent entering the workforce now have less first-hand experience engaging in ad hoc conversations on corded phones, striking up a conversation with someone in line for a movie ticket, or talking to a pizza delivery person to get change for orders. The accounts of those activities will become synonymous to the stories of walking to school in the snow uphill both ways or walking past a stray dinosaur on the way to work at Slate Rock & Grave (obscure Fred Flintstone reference).

The current and future generations of high school and college graduates will have only answered their *own* phones once they screened the caller. Going into a bank on a weekly basis? Definitely not.

It is *even* more dire for the *even* younger generations. Playing outside with friends became playing video games at a friend's house, changed further to now playing video games from our own house while our friends play from their houses. I can appreciate that there is some socialization in the form of banter over a headset, however, I think most would agree that it is still not quite the same.

There are plenty of folks still and already in the workforce with memories of home phones and restaurant reviews in person, but the increasing remote and digital experiences on a daily basis are slowly replacing those memories.

> *Certainly, the rise in populations studying and working from home and turning to hybrid models will have an impact on our society for many reasons. This flexibility has provided and will continue to provide positive implications, and it should be noted that virtual spaces and videoconferencing are fantastic alternatives to in-person interactions. However, the reduction of the chatter walking into workspaces in the morning, casual chats in breakrooms, and ad hoc debates in the hallways will leave its mark on our human interaction skills.*

2. Technology Replacements

As I've mentioned, technology is absolutely amazing. In many ways it's our human contribution to the planet. We don't see any other species coding or building robots, do we?

I would suggest, however, that our reliance on technology to provide support in areas where we are capacity constrained, has side effects.

Let's look at a common workplace example: a team developing a proposal.

In service-providing industries, global teams are often asked to prepare proposals based on a set of client requirements. These proposals often necessitate bringing together a diverse group of people with diverse backgrounds, skills, and areas of expertise to address the questions and put forward a solid response.

How advantageous it would be to bring this group of people together in person to focus on the requirements, brainstorm on white boards, and noodle on colorful sticky pads. The group could bring even more people to the room, if and when gaps emerge from the discussion. The energy would pulsate throughout the building.

This approach could work well and be applied successfully in a virtual setting with focused mindsets, leveraging both videoconferencing and virtual white boards and virtual stickies to capture ideas from the group in real time.

Instead, too often emails are relied upon to bring varying opinions together. We must know that sending an email to 15 people asking for perspectives toward a proposal will not yield the same outcome had those individuals been brought together live for a discussion. We should not expect the same creativity to surface. We should not expect the same active participation from the group.

How can we?

As I said, and I stand by this statement: technology is amazing. We look to robotic process automation to automate work activities. We rely on artificial intelligence to help us make recommendations and decisions. These tools are incredible.

These advancements put great pressure on us humans, which is good if we take advantage of the opportunities. We must not only implement the technologies but learn to work harmoniously with them to realize the full benefit of what these technologies can bring. One benefit is that often they free up human time which can then be redirected to focus on activities which humans can do better than any technology — our biggest area of differentiation from software or hardware. This area of differentiation, if we choose to recognize and nurture it, is our ability to be human and interact with other humans as humans.

3. Cross-discipline Collaboration Expected

How exciting is this time on our planet? We are cracking problems that seemed uncrackable. We are revolutionizing what we eat, how we breath, how we travel, how we pay for things, and generally how we live. How are we making these revolutionary changes?

The key ingredient to the disruption and transformation responsible for these radical changes is the necessity and ability to bring a variety of talents to the table.

Look at how we stay safe in our cars. Yes, we have seat belts and air bags, but let's look more deeply.

When we bring in the technologies around virtual reality to our newest of drivers in simulations, mistakes are made on a virtual road without the implications of a real mistake, resulting in a car accident.

When we bring in health and wellness features to cars, our car can sense by cardiac outputs and breathing rates if we're experiencing a medical emergency or predict that we may soon, so it alerts us to some recommended next steps, avoiding what could have become a real road emergency for us and other drivers and passengers in our path.

High tech and life sciences. Psychology and automobile prototyping. Blockchain and process optimization. It's a cross-industry, cross-domain, cross-skill world out there if we enable and empower it. It crosses disciplines.

And what happens when we bring these different disciplines together? We're in essence bringing together different styles, personalities, and cultures. Workplaces and work styles that matured in siloes are now coming together.

The outcomes expected should be revolutionary, but often the process can look more chaotic than smooth.

To make the kinds of advancements we believe *are* achievable requires healthy conversation and collaboration across and amongst the necessary diversities, beyond the first step of identifying and bringing those right minds together in a room — digital or otherwise.

4. Over-scheduled, Inefficient, and Ineffective

Wow, are we overscheduled.

In the workplace, we consider ourselves lucky if we're not managing each minute of the day at the mercy of our electronic calendar, which captures the choreography of our office time and our personal time, in 30-minute increments, if not shorter. Though it doesn't look or feel like the choreography of a ballet with movements fluid and graceful; it's more like the choreography of a march or a sprint, either rigid with harsh changes in direction or a chaotic or frantic accelerated pace incapable of truly acknowledging and therefore responding to the world around.

Let's take a closer look at an illustrative morning routine, from 8 to 8:30 a.m. we'll talk about our talent agenda, 8:30 to 10 a.m. we'll discuss the portfolio of work for the year, 10 to 10:30 a.m. a one-on-one to discuss a colleague's work-life balance (ironic), 10:30 to 11 a.m. time to review a proposal, 11 to 11:30 a.m. another one-on-one, 11:30 a.m. to noon, travel to another site. Forget lunch, someone scheduled a call right over that.

And we're lucky if we can allow ourselves to stick to that kind of schedule without too many double, triple, or quadruple bookings.

Try taking a face-to-face meeting while on an existing teleconference? Yes, that happened to me. A few years ago, I was scheduled in a meeting, but another team had to move their time with me, so I was attempting to accommodate everyone: the curse of the overlapping meetings. I told all participants in that train wreck of an afternoon that I was going to bounce back and forth with my attention, so my apologies in advance. Afterwards one of my team members commented that it was impressive when, in actuality, it was the opposite of impressive. It was clearly evident that I lost the battle with my schedule and brought that loss to everyone with me. I have always been an advocate for leadership that is present and for leaders who give their whole attention to what is in front of them. My dual meeting strategy was an epic failure and one I have not, nor would not let happen again.

We may find those overlapping discussions comical, maybe even ridiculous. But how many of us text during a meeting? For those moments, our mind is investing in other topics. Not too far off from being in a whole separate call altogether.

Let's assume we only have one discussion in a timeslot and aren't multi-tasking. How productive is that one discussion which is nestled in an overscheduled calendar multiplied by the number of people in the discussion also between their other back-to-back time commitments?

In case we would challenge this thinking, asserting that there is full productivity during each scheduled block of time, I would like to share with you how most back-to-back calls start. We can then make judgment on how productive this particular call is destined to be.

Illustrative: start of a team call starring fictitious leaders (though based on real personas) Mary, Robert, Rick, Susan, and David.

MARY: "Okay, team, let's get the innovating started as we only have 30 minutes."

ROBERT: "Okay, is Rick on yet?"

RICK: [unintelligible robot-like sound]

ROBERT: "Is that Rick?"

RICK: [unintelligible robot-like sound again]

ROBERT: "Rick, you should dial back in? We can't hear what you're saying."

RICK: [unintelligible robot-like sound]

ROBERT: "Rick, dial back in."

RICK: [unintelligible robot-like sound]

ROBERT: "Rick?"

RICK: [unintelligible robot-like sound]

ROBERT: "Dial back in! Is Susan there?"

SUSAN: "Hi guys, this is Susan. I couldn't hear Rick either." [background noise]

ROBERT: "Susan, we hear a lot of noise in the background."

SUSAN: "Yeah, I'm at the airport. I'm trying to mute myself, but it's not working."

ROBERT: "Okay, I'll try to mute you. Did that work?"

SUSAN: "Can you hear me?"

ROBERT: "Yes. (Tries again.) Did that work?"

SUSAN: "Hello? Hello, can you hear me?"

ROBERT: "Yes, it's not working."

RICK: "Hi guys, it's Rick, I'm back. I'm not sure what just happened there. I've been getting great reception all day. Earlier today though it wasn't working when I had my first call at 7 a.m., but then it worked just fine. I had a call with Susan earlier before she took a flight, and I couldn't hear her very well with the background noise, but my line seemed to work okay. Maybe it has to do with the upgrade that happened on my computer overnight; I'm not sure what exactly was upgraded. Is Mary on?"

> *I'm all for sharing and storytelling, I really am, and I also tell quite a bit of personal anecdotes and stories myself. But come on, Rick!*

MARY: "Yes, I've been on."

DAVID: "Mary, where are you? Are you in the office? I'm taking the call from the A-2345 conference room."

MARY: "I'm here in my office, but let's go ahead and get started."

DAVID: "No, it's okay, I'll come to your office so we can take this call together."

ROBERT: "Guys, I need to drop five minutes early."

SUSAN: "Oh, yeah, I probably need to leave in about 10 minutes anyway to catch my flight."

RICK: [unintelligible robot-like sound]

ROBERT: "Rick, we don't hear you anymore."

5. Bye, Bye Thinking Time

Our color-coded calendar is filled with back-to-back discussions (hopefully not all starting like Mary, Rick, Robert, David, and Susan's call), and it is likely for many that these discussions cover a very disconnected set of topics.

Where is the thinking time so we can bring the best out of ourselves each day and know enough to think about how to bring the best out of others?

I had a conversation with a colleague the other day about how to book thinking time into our daily routine.

He insists blocking time every morning for 20 minutes allows him to get organized for the day, putting him into a more "proactive" mentality to approach his meetings with thoroughness and thoughtfulness. Most people, even those who block that time, would undoubtedly admit that they often give that time up as soon as a pressing matter or really any matter surfaces. The blocked time simply doesn't get the priority.

We can do ourselves great justice by booking the thinking time, at least trying, but what happened to the thinking time in between activities? While watching our kids' soccer games? Waiting for our tennis court time? Waiting in line to get into the theatre? We have become quick to turn to and pick up a device to check on emails, check our calendars, check the news, or check out a new game. We continue to squeeze out any thinking time from anywhere it used to pop up comfortably, naturally, and frequently.

We used to take time to just think. Be still. Where are we today? I'd challenge others: when they find themselves in the aforementioned situations, how quickly do they itch for their phone, tablet, connected watch, or another device? Even writing this one paragraph, I have checked my own device four times: the weather report, my email account, my calendar, and three incoming text messages. It's madness. Whiplash for the brain, and we find it difficult to stop ourselves.

How often have we been in a situation with others — waiting for something or in between events — forgotten our device, and can't believe the rudeness of others as they mentally take a journey away from the space we're sharing with them and enter into the virtual reality of a social media platform, news update, texting, or just searching the cast of *Fresh Prince of Bel Air* to see what they are up to these days?

Truly there is not much difference between standing with someone who is engaged in their device and standing alone.

So, what's missing? The thinking. Connecting our own thoughts to what happened earlier in the day or with plans for the future. Generations will no longer achieve the benefits of simply being still. Imagine how many of today's inventions and advancements were born during those moments. People learned how to process information, take the time to mentally explore concepts and build upon them. Then reengage with the world, perhaps with something reimagined. Without that time, the missed value is beyond measure.

More and more professionals have entered and are entering into this compromised work environment without the thinking time and human interaction boot camp of years ago, replaced by distracting devices and text conversations. We are preparing ourselves for a creative lull.

6. The Lids

Ah, the Lids. This could take a while. It could merit its own full chapter, but it belongs here. First, I'd like to state my belief that being a Lid is a transient state of mind versus permanent condition, but I invite you to form your own opinion.

Lids are not new to the workplace, but Lid-like behavior has become more prevalent the more radical ideas are born. However, let me define what I have coined the term "Lid" before I get ahead of myself.

A Lid in the workplace environment is someone who can shut down the room and not in a good way. This person doesn't let ideas bubble out, doesn't give oxygen to new ideas. A Lid is an innovation killer or at least an idea constrainer.

Have you ever been in a room with a team, and the creativity is bubbling over, ideas are proliferating, and filling the space? Have you seen a person being energized by another person and that person being energized by another and so on and so on — innovative thinking is all around? You know what this looks and feels like. Inspiring. Exciting. Contagious, positive energy.

How often have we all been in that situation which then becomes constrained by someone in the room who can't help but to negate the thinking, telling everyone why the ideas will not work, could not possibly work, and have never worked before? This is an individual who contributes to the discussion by explaining why the current leadership, environment, talent, and market all point to stagnation and status quo.

I refer to that person as a "Lid," someone who has the ability to stifle, restrict, and otherwise suck all oxygen out of a room (real or virtual). This is quite a power we give to a Lid. A Lid can destroy even the most excited of teams. A 120-minute brainstorm session can be killed by a Lid within only moments — if we let that happen.

I have seen Lids in action, and it is quite impressive. But *again*, not in a good way.

Let me explain what it can be like to share the space with a Lid. I'll describe an interaction as though it is currently happening.

I enter a conference room filled with colleagues. We start talking about completely new ways of running a part of a business. We outline the issues and reasons or root causes behind those issues. We then discuss which individuals and skills already are in the organization, just perhaps not being fully utilized; some of those individuals are in the room.

We then stand up, draw out new activities to optimize hand-offs and capture how technology can support those activities, uninhibited by the company's policies, historical precedence, and functional siloes. We now observe the Lid, circling the situation, just waiting for the chance to pounce (verbally).

Once we draw up these new activities and step back to look at the masterpiece, folks begin commenting on various parts to make further improvements or provide clarification. Some of those comments are:

- *"We should have a template so we can collect the same information at this point in time."*

- *"What if we skipped these three steps altogether; I don't know why we do them today anyway. That way, we'll get to a second iteration faster."*

The room buzzes with ideas; some people can't even stay seated in their chairs. I am one of those people. Folks roam around the room, looking at what we put together from different angles.

Then the Lid can no longer contain themself. The Lid must speak up. There it goes. It is difficult to say in which order these comments were forced upon the room, but the Lid says something like this.

- *"We can't possibly ask people around the world to capture information in the same way."*

- *"They have been working their own way for years."*

- *"How can you possibly think we'll get our external parties to buy in?"*

- *"We're never going to get our internal policies updated in time for the next round."*

- *"Far smarter people have been trying to fix these problems for years; what makes you think we can change anything here?"*

- *"We'll never get cross-functional agreement, which is the only way this had a shot, which it doesn't."*

- *"This probably won't work since we tried something like this before."*

- *"We tried this exact thing before, it didn't work."*

- *"No one else in the industry does it this way."*

- *"Everyone else does it this way — what's so innovative?"*

- *"This is too transformative to get done here. This isn't transformative at all."*

One can summarize the type of feedback, which a Lid may provide a room suggesting new ideas in five ways:

Lid Framework Categories	Example Statements
Historical confidence	"We tried that before; we did that before: it doesn't work."
Present confidence	"That doesn't work here; that won't work here."
False positivity angle	"That might work somewhere else (sounds positive), but not here."
Internal blame	"We don't have the culture to do that; that won't work because of our culture."
Lid deflection	"That could work but [insert another Lid name] won't go for it, doesn't like change."

So, ask yourself, have you known someone who has acted like a Lid? Have you acted like a Lid yourself? It's okay; awareness is the first step.

I continue, and will continue to contend, that a Lid can be a transient state of mind, and when the behavior is acknowledged, it can be managed.

We conclude our Lid scene by asking, "What harm could all those Lid statements have on a room filled with such optimism, positivity, and creativity?"

The answer is: significant harm. However, not *irreversible* harm.

Given the pervasiveness of the Lids across industries, across levels, across geographies even outside the workplace, it is worth taking a pause to ask how we can transform Lid behavior or at least contain it. How do we keep Lid behavior at bay and allow groups to continue along positive pathways of discussion and collaboration? To start, let's consider and apply the following three steps:

1. Bring awareness to the Lid behavior responsibly and respectfully.
2. Hold a smart sidebar with the individual expressing Lid-like sentiments.
3. Consider when and if a rational close to the meeting is needed.

1. Awareness

As I mentioned, I remain unconvinced that being a Lid is in one's genotype or phenotype. Lids are not hard-wired nor hard-coded. They are not afflicted necessarily with a permanent Lid state, either, since I've seen the converted. However, and for some, it may be more of a chronic condition.

Be aware of whether the person is a repeat offender as a Lid or uncharacteristically acting like one. Are the conditions around this person (e.g., overscheduled, stretched across too many activities, having a rough day) such that those explain why the behavior is manifesting itself around us at that time?

Is this person ready to be in this discussion? Ready to allow the team to feel safe in an improvised exchange of thought? If not, it may be time for that person to be excused or for the meeting to be cut short, continued at another time, on another day, or with an updated group of attendees. All acceptable answers.

However, in the situation where the conversation must continue, and once we are aware of someone behaving like a Lid, we, as well as others around us, have the power to override the Lid. But how?

- Be aware of what questions are asked of someone behaving like a Lid.
    - Instead of asking completely open-ended questions like, "When can we have this report," consider asking questions that are rooted in the possible. Try, "How could we work as a team to get the report finished on time or even ahead of schedule?"
    - Instead of, "Do you think they'll value the meeting," try, "What would an amazing meeting look like? How do we want them to feel? How can we keep them energized and engaged? What outcomes would make the team feel like it was a productive day and a good use of time?"
- Be aware of how to receive comments that are positive, productive, and constructive, showing people that positivity is welcome in this space.
    - Appreciate those comments and that contribution.
    - Thank those who build up ideas versus knock them down. We respond this way with children when a good deed is witnessed, focusing on and calling out positive behaviors, why not in the workplace? "Timmy, thank you for sharing your graham crackers with Pat. Maybe next time you won't drop them on the ground first, but

it's a very nice thought you had there, Timmy. Very much appreciated."

- Be aware of how to receive comments that constrain the thinking by embracing before pivoting.
  - o In other words, it may be that a Lid predictably shares how an idea couldn't possibly work. Welcome those words by saying something like, "It might not work, that's true. Let's brainstorm ways in which it could — even if those ideas are way out there in terms of feasibility. All ideas are good ones, let's put together a list that we can evaluate later."
  - o No sense in shooting down the shooter of ideas. We'll just start to look like a Lid, and no one wants that.

2. Smart Sidebar with the Lid

It is possible that a Lid can be too tight, meaning that the Lid is not budging in how the Lid is approaching the discussion. We tried the approaches above, and those did not seem to work. It may be time to elicit some advice or help. The best person to help with the Lid? The Lid. It's time to pull the Lid into a sidebar (i.e., off to the side) chat.

When possible, and in a non-threatening, non-finger-pointing way, step aside with the Lid. This can be done virtually through instant messaging or physically by walking to another part of the space. It's time to be honest with the Lid. Those in the room are trying to be positive, creative, and idea-generating versus inhibited. How can the Lid help allow the room to continue in that way? How can the Lid help bring out the best from the room? Has the Lid noticed anyone else in the room who has been quiet? Non-productive? If so, you may need to pull that person into a smart sidebar as well for different reasons.

Most people want to be helpful and would welcome the opportunity to play the "hero" role of sorts so let the Lid help. Bring the Lid into the circle of trust. It may be just what the situation needs.

3. Rational Close

The meeting has come to an end. Ideas have been captured. We have avoided as many traps as we could that were set out by the Lids. Brains are sore from being hard at work. Those who shared ideas are feeling appreciated, as well as mentally fatigued.

It is time to close the meeting. This is a critical time to leave an inspiring message for the participants not only to properly wrap up, but also to promote positivity and constructive dialogue for the next meeting. This is the time to close rationally.

Close with the same energy that prevented the Lid from sucking it away.

"This has been a great discussion, and I appreciate your time, thoughtfulness, and bravery in sharing your ideas and willingness to hear what we all had to say. I'll summarize where we landed so we may pick up from here and continue to take this forward with the same focus and attention that was evident today."

This is not the time to shame anyone, knock anyone down, nor wish it had been better. It was what it was. The chapter has closed on this particular conversation. As long as there wasn't just one person in the room sharing, others deserve the gratitude. Chances are they'll then act similarly when they hold and close their next meeting. Consider that behaviors are very contagious. We try not to pick up the bad ones, and we try to pass along the good ones. It often takes discipline, and at times it takes "sidebars," but the time taken, and discipline applied are worth the reward.

So, we clearly have work to do in the workplace. We must clearly compensate for the lack of social interaction practice time in our daily lives.

We must learn to manage Lid behavior and prevent ourselves from falling into the same Lid traps. We must aim to bring out the best of ourselves and the best of one another in every conversation. Easy. Now on to how.

III

WORKPLACE TURNING TO IMPROV

Finding Improv

It's clear from the subject of this book that I believe improv, which in this case is an abbreviated way of referring to improvisational comedy specifically, is a key to unlocking how we can improve the workplace, making it better and more productive. However, what may not be clear is how I found improv and therefore can confidently assert this claim. Let's start from the very beginning.

I was born in Cincinnati, Ohio. Like many parents across the globe, most in the Midwest signed up their kids to play soccer, just hoping their child would tolerate it and maybe even like it. My parents were no different.

Midwestern parents smiled when their kids played with energy. They beamed when their kids wholeheartedly loved playing. And they watched as their kids demonstrated true talent both defensively and offensively. These parents and kids would drive to and from games imagining the soccer scholarships and professional opportunities. Very exciting!

This was not the reality for me nor for my parents.

I was not good at soccer. That might be an understatement. I was terrible at soccer. I don't want to toot my own horn, but it's possible I was one of the worst, which does put me in a rather elite group of soccer underachievers. I'm not suggesting I'm proud of this elite status, but it is worth noting — not everyone achieves this level of underperformance.

I loved going to games though, which you might not expect from such an elite soccer nightmare child. It wasn't because I was good at it, I wasn't. In case I wasn't clear, I wasn't good defensively, and I wasn't good offensively. Seriously, I didn't always know where the ball was on the field, so I certainly couldn't kick it anywhere intentionally. I loved the games since it meant I would stand on the big green field with lots of friends and new people. I would introduce myself and then talk to the kids on the other team. I would ask them questions about their schools, pets, summer camps, and families. I was fascinated that these kids lived similar, yet completely different lives with teachers I didn't know, schools I didn't know, and neighborhoods I didn't know. That was very exciting.

If you would have asked my dad about my soccer performance in the years that followed my soccer-playing days, he would have recalled that I wasn't that bad at soccer. He liked to tell a story of the game when I scored a goal. A few Thanksgivings ago, when we were all sitting around the dinner table, his story grew to include a part describing a time when I scored multiple goals. I assured him that this goal-filled game never happened. I never scored a goal, and I certainly didn't score a few, but he insisted. Therefore, I decided to let him hold onto that "memory" since it made him happy.

So, instead of soccer, my family and I decided to turn to entertainment and specifically the performing arts where I could work on skills that had a greater probability for improvement than my soccer skills. When most of my friends then continued to play soccer or baseball on Saturdays, I shifted my focus and time to the University of Cincinnati College Conservatory of Music where I took acting and dance classes. I spent my Saturdays not kicking a ball around the soccer field nor throwing a ball to home plate, but instead playing theatre games and doing scene work. I found my home on the stage.

When I was looking for a university that met my academic goals in science and the arts, I was fortunate to get accepted to Northwestern University where I majored in biomedical engineering with a theme in fine arts and happily took performance classes. I would also find theatre-related extracurriculars.

This was how I found improvisational comedy.

I had been doing improvised scene work for years in acting classes growing up, and I was able to bring that training to an improv comedy group.

With no specific comedy background, however, when I saw a flyer announcing auditions for an improv comedy group in the student union, I signed up.

Like so many college students, my confidence far outweighed my capability. I walked down campus, about 20 minutes from north campus to south campus, listening to Dave Matthews Band on my cassette player with this confidence. How did the audition go? It was the best and worst audition. It was the best audition because I rocked it. I did a scene, it was funny, people laughed, and I would find out later that I got in the group! I made the cast list. It was the worst audition since I would realize later, after I learned the rules of improv,

35

that I had broken the rules of improv in that audition. I'll share how I did that... *later*.

So, there I was, I made it in this improv group! Woo-hoo! See you all on the weekends for the shows. I mean, it's improv after all. Spontaneous, no preparing, rehearsing. I thought, *see you castmates at showtime*.

I was wrong.

In fact, we practiced every night, four hours a night. As an engineering student, this meant that after rehearsals, I headed back to my dorm around 12:30 a.m. to *begin* the next part of my evening: study time. I'd never complain about it though; I loved every part of it.

We performed two shows Friday night and two shows Saturday night in downtown Chicago. Sometimes we performed on campus and sometimes in other states. The experience had a major impact on me. I would never be the same. My personal and professional approaches to human interaction would never be the same, either.

Following graduation from Northwestern, I began my career in management consulting, and continued to build on it for more than 20 years now.

After only a few years observing how the workplace functions, I soon recognized the need for improv at work and started to bring improv into the conversation, proactively and reactively.

Proactively. During a week-long centralized training session, all participants had the optional opportunity to share a topic of their choosing for 15 minutes at a happy hour. Each topic was given space in a large conference room like at a college or career fair, and attendees would decide which topic to attend. Each topic owner was asked to run their 15-minute topic twice so attendees could rotate and experience two out of the 20 or so topics.

During the day, the sign-up sheet went around the training room several times. When I first saw the sign-up sheet, the topics already volunteered depressed me. So-and-so would talk about a software release. Another so-and-so signed up to talk about the impact of the new legislation on validation requirements. These were topics for a happy hour? I think not.

When the sign-up sheet came around for the fourth time, I decided to stop poking at the topics and added one to the list: improv in the office. I had no idea then exactly what I was going to do, but I knew it was relevant, leveraged my background, and was fun — with or without a drink in hand.

About 15 people came to my first 15-minute session. I shared my background, several improv rules, and how those rules were practiced in the improv setting. I then led the group in a theatre game intended to bring the rule to life for the workplace. The group was incredible. They lit up, showed up, and leaned in. Word got around and more than 50 people came to my second session. It became even more clear to me: there's something to this improv at work concept.

Reactively. When colleagues or supervisors found out about my background, I was often asked to entertain teams if we were waiting for something. At a team dinner while waiting for the entrées to be served, one of my colleagues stood up in front of the restaurant dining room and suggested that I come up and perform stand-up. I had never performed stand-up, but I was called upon to do something with my background, so I took advantage of the situation and brought improv to the salad course. On another day I was in a training class waiting for the guest speaker to arrive, and another colleague suggested the same of me. "Come up, Nicole, and do something funny." Seriously?!

I did not want to become the team circus pet. I'd say, "Not going to do stand-up — but let me talk about improv and why it's relevant in the workplace and then we'll practice together."

It is hard for me to believe that I have been at the same company for more than 20 years. Though nothing has been the "same" during that time. I have enjoyed working with thousands of people from a variety of companies and spent time designing and implementing completely different kinds of projects with varying sets of objectives, all aimed at improving businesses at the organizational and individual contribution levels.

During my career, I have come to value a set of principles about the workplace which would explain why I believe improv is needed in the work environment:

- Innovation is required in business.
- In order to succeed at innovation, it is important to bring collaboration.
- In order to achieve productive collaboration, it is important to excel at communication.
- The building blocks that make up innovation, collaboration, and communication can be found in our human interactions.
- Therefore, in order to innovate, collaborate, and communicate effectively, it is critical to optimize human interactions.

When it comes to the optimization of human interaction, we have a long way to go as a workforce. By sitting on project teams and leadership teams, as well as by being around other project teams and leadership teams as a spectator, I have seen what *really* good human interaction looks like. I've seen what really, *really* good interaction looks like. However, I also have seen what bad, *really* bad human interaction looks like. This made me pause and reflect.

Where have I spent time laser-focused on human interaction? Where is it critical to bring the best out of yourself and others for the purpose of bringing the best ideas to the surface and having the best experiences?

Improv.

I'm convinced that the workplace has a lot to learn from improv. And it's a good thing improv has a lot to teach.

What Is Improv

Throughout my career I've created and delivered countless presentations. One technique I've used and seen, repeatedly, is turning to the dictionary first when covering a new topic either in preparation or in the presentation itself. So, let's review several improv definitions, so you don't need to look it up yourselves. Yes, it is my pleasure to do this for you, and you are welcome.

Improv, according to *Merriam-Webster: of, relating to, or being improvisation and especially an improvised comedy routine.*

I absolutely would never criticize *Merriam-Webster*, though we might find a way to define improv without using the word itself in the definition two more times. But I digress.

Improv, according to Wikipedia: *Improvisation is the activity of making or doing something not planned beforehand, using whatever can be found.*

Improvisation, in the performing arts, is a very spontaneous performance without specific or scripted preparation.

I'm inspired. Let's also look at another definition. *My* definition.

Improv, according to me: *Improvisation, specifically successful improvisation, follows a considerable amount of preparation and is the practice of creating discussions and experiences in the moment where energy is unconstrained, creativity is unleashed, and the possibilities are unimaginable (in a good way).*

Workplace & Improv: Similarities

I once read: "Improvisation is really an example of heightened communication, relying on an actor's ability to engage completely with fellow performers, as well as their own character."

Imagine if this sentiment were approached in the workplace. We want to say, "Workplace interactions are really examples of heightened communication, relying on an executive's ability to engage completely with their colleagues and teams in addition to their own strengths."

Many of the principles applied in improvisational comedy hold true for the business world as well. In fact, the objectives of both worlds are rather similar. In both worlds, consider that the following tenets are true:

1. Resolution and outcomes are important.
2. Innovation is expected and measured.
3. Positive and negative energies are contagious, and each can impact performance and outcomes in either direction.
4. Experience is as important as outcomes.

1. Resolution and Outcomes are Important.

Being a senior leader working on many different industry challenges has had its advantages, disadvantages, as well as personal moments of insanity.

It has been priceless being part of cross-functional, cross-disciplined teams, focused on complex problems, with each person bringing different skills, yet all bringing the same desire to achieve common goals.

I have learned to have confidence through ambiguity and have become a big fan of the phrase, *we* will figure this out. *We* will get to the other side, eventually look back, and smile at the journey *we* all took together with pride that *we* didn't give up too quickly. *We* stuck with it. *We* stuck with each other.

It took years, however, of feeling uncertain at the beginning of an ambiguous situation, and emerging at the end positively, to come to the conclusion that *we* will figure it out. For one project when I was more junior in my career, my team was tasked to cut a business metric by 50 percent. Without even looking at the details, a goal was set — cut by 50 percent. I felt uncertain. Would we figure out how that could be possible? Surely smarter people have thought about how to make this happen. How will we suddenly figure out how to cut it by 50 percent? Did I mention the goal was *50 percent?* The thought crossed my mind, *Maybe we are collectively just too human, too ordinary, too rooted in today's constraints to crack this one and hit this goal.* Remember how much we were supposed to reduce this metric — *50 percent.* It didn't matter that the task was daunting, the outcome desired was clear to all of us. We quickly left that uncertainty on the figurative curb and approached the situation with the belief that we'd figure it out, and we did.

In addition to delivering on tasks and projects, another part of the business world is selling stakeholders on an idea of doing a new thing or stopping an organization from doing another thing. A person or team may have a vision, may put together an incredible business case outlining why that vision is critical for the organization. That person or team may bring all the best approaches, methods, templates, timelines, and estimated cost to do that work. That person or team may sit with various stakeholders over a few weeks' time to present why the recommended path is the right one for the organization. And after all that productive time bringing people together to shape the thinking, the stakeholders say no. The work itself isn't enough to declare a team victory; the outcomes were not achieved.

The business world is a place that clearly appreciates hard work and values those who do that hard work. However, that appreciation does not necessarily mean the hard work alone is rewarded. What is valued more than hard work is the "so-what" part.

The "so-what" part can be found in the results and the outcomes.

After all that hard work, *so what?* Did we achieve our objective for the business and are we then faster, smarter, better? Are we growing the business? Are we able to hire more people, expand our scope of services, reach more people, and/or reach the right diversity of people? What value are we delivering to our people, our teams, our clients, our customers, our shareholders, as well as stakeholders?

What does this have to do with improvisational comedy? *Everything.*

In an improvised scene on the stage, the actors organically create a situation, an issue, a challenge, or an opportunity and build a journey with a resolution. How do they get from issue to outcome? How do they get to the point in a scene when they call "scene" (which means the scene ended) in a way that the audience feels satisfied?

There should be closure, preferably good closure. It is along that journey where the actors have fun, sure they can go off on tangents. They have fun with the audience. However, deep inside, very deep, they know that at some point they will be expected to find some sort of purpose for what they're doing up on that stage and give the audience resolution. They aim to achieve some sort of outcome, perhaps sillier than outcomes in the business world, and point to closure. Then the audience should deliver the outcome expected of them, hopefully, if all went well; the outcome could be audibly identified as laughter and applause. As I said, *hopefully.*

For both the business world and improv comedy world, results and outcomes are critical for success. And in both cases, practice and experience bring the confidence necessary to achieve those results and outcomes with greater probability of success.

2. *Innovation is Expected and Measured.*

Speaking of innovation, before it can be expected and measured, what foundation should be put in place?

In improv, the expectation is that the audience is watching something that has never happened before: true innovation.

How sad for an audience member walking out of an improv show to say, "The show was okay, but I've heard those jokes before. Same old, same old."

If the content is to be new and exciting for each performance, my friends would ask me, "Why do you rehearse so much with your improv group? What are you rehearsing if it's not lines in a script?"

Most rehearsal time for improv is spent simply practicing a variety of scenes with different combinations of cast members, as well as playing improv games to practice and master the rules of improv. Most importantly, rehearsal time is intended to increasingly build confidence to perform more effectively on stage as an individual and as a cast.

It's like weight training for an Olympic sport in the weight room. An athlete weight trains to get stronger. An athlete weight trains to later be able to apply that strength towards their sport. I'm not a professional athlete — I made that point earlier — but I do know that there are many similarities among a stage performer, athlete, and businessperson.

One commonality is that what makes it possible to perform and bring your best to a "Moment that Matters" (e.g., show, game, meeting) is in fact the work that went into that activity before the moment in the spotlight: on a stage, on a field, or in a boardroom.

For an improv actor, performing in a scene on the stage, those skills (i.e., building blocks) require flexing and growing with confidence to innovate and go in all directions, with an engaged audience. This takes the *audience* to places they could not have imagined and places the *performer* could not have imagined. The actor's neural pathways must be open to process new ideas, forge into new territories, and explore new adventures on stage with fellow actors.

In other words, if innovation is expected, it should then also be expected that the group of actors have fine-tuned their capabilities to lead to that innovation. Everyone in the group must learn not only how to be an innovative thinker, but also how to encourage innovation from others: how to both generate ideas and welcome or expand upon the ideas of others.

Leading to the important question, why do we not take this approach with ourselves and our teams in business?

For specific work objectives, we put teams together with an expectation to be innovative and then we expect that innovation without the necessary practices and rules to achieve that innovation. We insufficiently cover workplace training topics such as: optimizing human interactions, sharpening wits in conversations, and building confidence to carry into the workplace environment. There is no innovation muscle to flex. There is no creativity credit in the creativity bank from which to make a withdrawal when it is time to innovate. There is no rehearsal time dedicated to the how, only the expectation of the what: innovation.

We're simply not prepared.

We should instead invest time in supporting our teams as they learn, grow, and develop an innovation mindset which can then be applied, freed, and leveraged to explore ideas.

Instead, we treat innovation like something you can buy in a supermarket.

"I need some innovation with a half pound of extra lean roast beef."

"I forgot to mention, I'll need that innovation now."

It doesn't work that way, sadly.

Now, there *is* plenty to be said about innovation and plenty that *has* been said. I want to highlight a critical point about innovation. Before I do though, please take a deep breath in.

Now, please. Take a deep breath in. This is not a test.

I mean it, deep breath. *You*. Right now.

If you're the type of person who took that deep breath the first time I asked for it, well, thank you and also feel free to take another one or two deep breaths.

What I must highlight on innovation is this: innovation comes when we and our brains are able and allowed to operate on a calmer plane. When a sense of panic is not felt. When pressure is not felt.

When we and our brains have been led to believe, or fundamentally do believe, that we both can accomplish anything, then we and our brains have some reason to believe that the creativity process is real and valued.

Without those beliefs within a calm mindset (preferably while taking those deep breaths, every once in a while), it is just as though we and our brains are being told "Innovate now, now, now, now." How does that feel? It is unlikely that approach will yield some great return. It is unlikely that approach is going to allow us to bring the best out of ourselves, our brains, our teams, and their brains.

Once our mindset is in a good place, that's step one.

Interesting that innovation in the improv world is measured by the ability to touch an audience member in a new way, typically eliciting an immediate reaction: laughter. In the business world, we work a little bit harder to measure impact: studies, surveys, and scorecards. We ask, "How are we doing bringing innovation to you?" Then, those responding must think back to which ideas were brought to them.

Another way to think about it would be, how innovative is the environment? Are new ideas brought up in conversation, then discussed and received? Are forums, sessions, and roundtables set up frequently to explore ideas together? Seems to me we need to change the playing field in terms of how we measure success around innovation. We need to welcome, appreciate, and implement new ideas and not just count them up for an annual scorecard. If we made those adjustments, the value would be astronomical as would be the business value.

3. Positive and Negative Energies are Contagious, and Each can Impact Performance and Outcomes in Either Direction.

"Hi Alan, how are you?"

Easy enough way to start off a meeting. Generic opening. Obligatory question. But what comes next? Innately, I personally, typically, and sincerely answer that question with an enthusiastic positive response — "Great" — *and why not?*

If I'm working, I'm well enough to work and isn't that something to be happy about? On days when I'm not as well, people get a less cheerful response, I suppose, as they should. Why are we even in a meeting together when I'm not feeling well today?

But, most days, I find it inspiring to be around positive people and prefer to bring that energy to those around me as well. I choose that. Just as you choose what energy *you* bring to those around *you*. Everyday. No need to skip around the room if that's not authentic to your style, no need to talk about rainbows and unicorns specifically, but you might bring some enthusiasm to the very first exchange of pleasantries.

How do you normally answer that question?

I recently spent a week consciously answering with a very upbeat response to that question and each time, got a smile or chuckle in return. Then, I'd ask: "How are you?" and rarely got back anything less enthusiastic.

And that's just the beginning of how anyone can contribute positive energy to conversation.

A few years ago, I worked with an industry leader who made it seem as though any challenge, big or small, could get resolved. He would bring a rather large group together into a conference room, present an issue we had to tackle, and never once did I get the sense that this group wouldn't be able to tackle it. He might laugh at an idea or two, but not in a discouraging way, rather in a "maybe" way such that we didn't think it was a terrible idea, just not a fully baked one yet. *Yet* being an important word. We'd get there. We'd figure it out.

This environment changes how teams step up and lean into an issue. This positivity vibe brings the team together. We're in this together. It also creates a sense of optimism. We'll get there together.

Why are most improvisational comedians having more fun in their day than the typical businessperson?

Let's be honest. It is likely that many factors provide explanation. A key reason must be that the improv actor enters their "work" with a certain belief that things will go well on stage; there will be smiles, there will be laughter, there will be fun. With that backdrop, yes, then improvisational comedians apply techniques to support optimal interactions and entertaining experiences for themselves, their audiences, and they use games to reinforce those techniques. Thus, our journey into this world continues.

4. *Experience is as Important as Outcomes.*

As I have heard and shared with my own children, "It is not whether you win or lose, it is how you play the game."

It seems obvious to say when watching kids play a board game. We want our kids to play how we want them to live with integrity and kindness.

The statement is less obvious and inconsistently believed in the workplace when at times it seems as though the outcomes are the only things that matter.

In the improv world, for actors and the audience, the experience is the show, and that show leads to the outcome of laughter, enjoyment, and hopefully a better sense of feeling in that day. Happy. Less stressed. Simply stated, feeling good.

For the improv actor specifically, however, it is possible to have had a negative experience on stage though the outcome for the audience remains great and achieved: laughter and applause. Maybe even a standing ovation.

Shouldn't life really allow for more standing ovations, in everyday settings? Just saying what we're all thinking.

Back to the actor. Bad experience, good outcomes. For example, the actor could have experienced any of the following:

- Neglected on stage by another performer. Ouch.
- Got tongue-tied and lost the train of thought. Ouch.
- Fell on stage. *Real* ouch.

From those experiences, the actor may decide not to work with this improv cast again, in that theatre, or worse, they decide to quit improv altogether because they became insecure about their own ability to articulate dialogue. In this example, the experience, or rather negative experience, overshadowed the outcomes. Significantly.

In work settings, it is also clear how experience may overshadow outcomes.

Let's look at two teams working on a presentation for an executive committee. Each team mobilizes and executes steps to put the various parts of the presentation together, presents the presentation, and then notes the outcome. An outcome may be buy-in from the executive committee with funding to allow the team to continue its work or an outcome may be a request to pause the work or even discontinue indefinitely.

Team One
Team One mobilizes with a kick-off meeting where the senior team leader stands in the center of the room, speaking at the newly gathered team members and invokes fear in the group unnecessarily.

"Thanks for being here today. Since there's a lot to get done, we don't have time for each person to introduce themselves, so I sent out a chart with everyone's picture, along with their area of expertise. Please note that this is an incredibly important time for this team; don't screw it up."

The team starts to break into sub-teams to bring the various parts of the presentation together over a defined timeframe. When those sub-teams report status to the other sub-team leads and the senior team leader, the progress reports often get verbally beaten up.

"What is this? This doesn't make any sense. Why aren't you further along? Is anyone even proofreading your work? How much time did you put into this before showing up today?"

It becomes clear to the team members that the team mentality is rooted in the saying, "Save yourself" which creates finger pointing, berating team members behind the scenes, and self-doubt running amuck.

Team Two

Team Two starts up very differently. The team comes together and does a proper set of introductions, getting to know each other personally, as well as professionally. They share new facts and their areas of expertise, as well as what they would like to accomplish from this activity. They learn new information about each other, information that will serve them well throughout the project.

"Hi, my name is Mary. I'm from Chicago, and I live there with three dogs who probably would be happier if I moved out so they could have true run of the place. I'm an expert in technology projects and bring a well-researched eye to that activity. I'm excited about the concept of this presentation since I think we could do something of real value here and can't wait to articulate that value through the numbers in a business case. I've spent a lot of time building out these types of business cases, to which I'm also excited to contribute — but I haven't spent much time in pulling these types of presentations together end-to-end. So, I hope to spend time with other parts of this team to learn, as well as contribute."

The fact is, had Mary not been asked to answer all those introductory questions, would she have shared that information? Would the team have known what she wanted to learn from the team and the experience? Would they have included her in parts of the effort that didn't squarely relate to her specific area of expertise? By taking this time and focusing on the individuals who are part of the team, the experience for each team member already is set up better for success.

The team members look at one another and hear from each other. There doesn't seem to be a hierarchy here — the team is focused on the best possible presentation for an executive review.

Along the way for this team, new ideas are embraced. The team keeps a log so that there's focus on what is happening, but with the recognition that it is still vital to capture new ideas for review when the team can take the time.

Sub-team progress meetings are held for those sub-teams to share; they brainstorm resolutions to small issues along the way. They discuss what else each sub-team could be doing to optimize overall team performance. The team environment was established as a safe space, so team members speak up and are not afraid to discuss a hiccup or concern since the rest of the team is supportive. The team mentality of "All for one, one for all" abounded.

After each team developed presentations and presented, what are the most important questions to ask? It is interesting to note whether or not each of these teams was funded for next steps, true. And they were (in this fictitious scenario where anything can happen).

It may be more important to ask how the team member's experience as a part of the team would shape their own next steps.
- Who is more likely to bring new ideas into situations?
- Who is more likely to want to work with this team again?
- Who is more likely to inspire the next team?

- Who is more likely to want to stay at that company?

Experiences stick with us. Experiences can make us feel fulfilled, respected, and happy. Experiences can also make us feel belittled, insecure, and unsettled.

What experiences are you creating for yourself and those around you?

IV

GETTING IMPROV STARTED
IN THE WORKPLACE

Preparation

We have covered why the business world requires more focus on building up human interaction skills. We covered the similarities between the business and improv worlds. We also covered how we can then apply and benefit from the lessons of improv to business. This takes preparation, however.

In the world of business transformation, we use workshopping as an approach to bring ideas and people together in order to ideate, discuss, and align. Assigning pre-work is a great way for folks to get their heads around a topic in advance of the session itself. By doing so, those folks tend to feel more comfortable in the session having had a few moments to themselves to process the information, formulate their own thinking, and become slightly more prepared than showing up unprepared.

Though it may seem as though improv is about operating under more spontaneous conditions, preparation is key as it allows the actor to set aside the time to sharpen one's skills and build the confidence required to apply the necessary techniques with a free mind. It is for this reason that preparation is necessary to explore improv techniques in the business setting.

Here you go. You are about to embark on a journey either by yourself, with a colleague, or with your team(s). It is exciting and a step towards a more collaborative, positive, and inspiring future, not to mention a great deal of fun. There also may be a bit of apprehension given that professionals are not necessarily accustomed to having this kind of fun at work.

"I don't want to embarrass myself; what if I do?"

"What if I don't know what to say?"

"What if I say something stupid?"

Here's the secret and the reality: Most people are far more concerned with themselves and their own performance than anyone else. This means everyone is asking those questions in their heads; they could not possibly be equally as focused on your contributions.

> *This narcissistic spirit serves everyone well here since each person can carry this calming mantra: no one is really paying all that much attention to me; I'll go for it.*

Scooping it out like an ice cream cone

Most acting students can recall a time in their early theatre educational days when they were forced to morph into inanimate objects. "Be an ice cream cone." There were logical reasons behind such requests. One reason in particular that I appreciated was that by "being an ice cream cone," you must completely step outside of yourself.

> *For those who never had to stand in front of an acting class and act like an ice cream cone, be grateful. It taught a good lesson but felt incredibly — let's just say — it felt as embarrassing as you can imagine it would.*

To become an ice cream cone, you can't simply pretend to be a version of yourself two years ago or two years in the future. You're not being asked to be a police officer or a teacher, role models you've seen over the course of your whole life.

You are asked to step into the role of an ice cream cone. How would it feel? As an ice cream cone, what are your dreams, fears, likes, and dislikes? What do you envy? What does a good day look like for you? You must abandon whatever social norms you know, your feelings, your behaviors, your preferences, and motivations — and try to understand the life of an ice cream cone.

So, be an ice cream cone. You can take that as literally or conceptually as you like. You've already shown great bravery by being a part of the movement to transform the workforce, simply because you're reading this book. I'm already very proud of you.

Take back the workforce — make it a place where people are free to bring the best and most unique parts of themselves to the conference room, the boardroom, or the virtual work room.

Read these rules, run these exercises with a colleague or with your team — make the improvisational techniques and games your own. Modify them. Maybe there are elements that are embarrassing to you at first. Ask yourself why. Step outside your normal approaches. Imagine how the application of these practices can unleash a new you, a new team, a new vibe, not to mention a new way of working.

According to some, improv comedy must be based on the following key principles: openness, optimism, and guts. It takes some guts. You may not really ask people to be ice cream cones, though it may feel like that is what you're doing to some.

My eyes were opened when I asked a group of professionals from around the world to play an improv game with one another — where the games would be played in small groups in front of the larger group. They didn't all jump up and down with excitement. I was shocked.

There was tremendous fear on their faces. I couldn't even get some of them to look me in the eye, so obviously, they didn't want to participate. I had underestimated their reaction. Having been in theatre classes myself from a young age and having a higher threshold for embarrassment than normal, I assumed the group would share my excitement for doing something completely different. I also assumed there would be the bellowing of laughter. This was not the case.

Instead, they looked horrified. I hadn't set it up well. I hadn't really set it up at all — I was so excited to share these games with this group of leaders. As I stood at the front of the room, looking at them, I realized I would have to step into each scene game we played, so they could always lean on me. I realized in fact that some of these games are best played in small groups, without a larger audience watching, until the folks in the room became more comfortable with the games and each other. I have since adjusted my own approach to include this type of a setup and can say happily that this adjustment has made all the difference.

As you think about how you'll engage with these rules, games, and activities, I will give you options based on the comfort levels you're observing in your room with your teammates. I will say, based on bringing these games to many more leaders, often some small baby steps into these activities will be all it takes for them to let down their guards, have fun, and pick up and run with these rules for the workplace.

Go

Time to get started.

When is the right time to get started working on human interaction skills such that you and your teams can realize the benefits in the workplace? Yesterday isn't an option.

That would be — now. *Now* is the time.

As previously outlined, the workplace is only becoming more and more complicated. All of us who enter the workplace each day are leaning more and more on technology to speak for us. Every day it becomes more and more important to create meaningful experiences in the workplace to grow businesses and grow careers.

Getting started is both the easiest and hardest part individually, as well as with your teams. You took the first step: you're reading about it. A most perfect start.

Here's the flow.

Seven critical improv rules for the workplace will be covered. Each rule will be explored in both improv and workplace environments. Next a few options to practice that rule will be described in the form of games or activities. Take notes when you're reading through these sections to make them your own — consider capturing where and when you might introduce these games, whom you might invite and what tweaks you would make to the activity. Use these activities before a big group presentation or during a team brainstorming event around a particular focus area or use them in a regularly scheduled team meeting to train your brain in a comfortable setting before you're in a "Moment that Matters."

Keep this book on your desk or even in your car as a reference; grab it if your team is spending a few hours together or even if there's just an extra 15 minutes of downtime. Take time to debrief after you employ one of the activities. It is the work during and between the activities that sharpen the skills, so whenever, however: take the time and make the time.

At the end of the book, we'll review how you might approach the activities with your teams over time.

In the improv world, a cast prepares all the time, as long as there is a cast, and there are shows for which to prepare. This should be the same in the workplace as well. This training process is anything but once and done. Please continue to revisit and/or alter the games based on how the teams are doing and based on what they can handle as they get more advanced. As long as there are reasons to communicate better, collaborate more effectively, and expect meaningful and innovative results, there's reason to prepare and work with the rules of improv.

Please consider the following requests of your team members who will join you to engage in bringing these improv rules and activities into the workplace:

- Understand the current and emerging complexities in the workplace and reliance on innovation, collaboration, and communication to achieve business success.
- Take a moment to think about the human interactions that have been and continue to be replaced by the non-verbal word, acronym, or emoticon.
- Reflect on the improv world and its reliance on successful human interactions.
- Now, come with an open mind and comfortable clothing to practice the art of human interaction as practiced in the improv world.
- Be ready to have fun!

Up next: the rules.

V

THE WARM UP TOGETHER AND ENERGIZE RULE

Overview: What's the rule?

Before you begin working on a meaningful topic with a small group or large team, take time to warm up together. This warm-up should not be optional and can include vocal, mental, and/or physical activities, to establish rapport, open neural pathways, build a level of trust, and have a little fun together. You'll actually feel the impact of the warm-up in the more comfortable team environment that is created, an environment that enables ideas to flow more easily once the work begins. This warm-up can be simple or more complex and may not require any preparation ahead of time other than planning to preserve that time in your schedules and picking which warm-up to do.

In improv: How does it work in improv comedy?

Before an improv comedy show, objectives and desired outcomes are clear to the performers: to have an awesome show where the actors are respected on stage and are having a great time, while the audience is enjoying themselves and preferably laughing.

One key to ensure an awesome show is showing up as a cast, with chemistry, which the audience then interprets as a group of people, who, dare I say it, *like* each other and has a high level of comfort with one another.

If the actors have performed as a cast over time and have rehearsed for weeks, months, or even years, that chemistry may have developed through sweat equity. Before the show, to ensure the team will perform as a well-oiled machine, they warm up, both individually and as a group.

An individual's warm-up is important to their individual performance. That actor might sit in a quiet space backstage, close their eyes, think about some affirming messages (*I can do this, I got this*) and perhaps meditate. That actor might also do some physical warm-ups with stretching or personal vocal warm-ups, moving their vocal range up and down the musical scale.

The cast must warm up together as well to gel as a group, work through any nervous kinks, and realize collectively that each actor is there to support one another throughout the entirety of the show. There's no thinking like: *I'll do my part, you do yours.* The team is in it together. They have one another's back.

What if the actors are coming together for the first time to perform? Or a guest actor is joining an established cast for the day? It is for these situations when warming up together becomes even more important. It is critical that the actors spend those minutes before a performance, together as a team, building comfort and familiarity, so that once performing, there is trust felt by both the actors and the audience.

Personally, before a show, I appreciated the time spent warming up and getting energized with my fellow castmates. We warmed up before *every* show — in fact before any type of acting — even at the start of an acting class.

We took that time to engage in a few activities, warm up vocally, mentally, and physically.

Actors share this commitment to warming up with other groups of performers or athletes on any stage or on any field. Most singers, dancers, or football players wouldn't dream of skipping a warm-up.

> *Can you imagine the Choir of King's College starting a performance without warming up? Can you imagine the New England Patriots or Cincinnati Bengals (shout out to Cincinnati) not warming up before a game?*

Performers and athletes prioritize the warm-up time individually to get in the right mindset and to be physically and mentally ready for what's to come. They prioritize that time as a cast or team, like an improv cast, recognizing the value of that time to start the performance journey together, as a unified front.

At the start of one of my improv performances, the audience was asked for a location suggestion to start a scene, and someone screamed out, "the nervous system." So, my fellow actors and I in a moment's notice became neurons. We ran around, created a conflict, and resolved that conflict. And we were ready. We had warmed up individually; we had warmed up together. We energized together and were ready to tackle just about anything. We may not have predicted that we would become part of a physiological movement that day on stage, but together we were ready for just about anything.

Wait, one might ask what about warming up *with* the audience before an improv show? Consider this visual. A dark theatre. A lone spotlight comes onto the stage. A somewhat nervous young man enters stage left and heads to the middle of the stage. All eyes on him. How does he create a relationship with the audience? It might be as easy as starting the conversation with the audience in seats. He might say:

"How are you all doing tonight?"

"Can I just say, I had the worst drive over tonight and am pretty sure there's a cop on Route 202 still looking for me." Some crazy story would then follow.

It's so simple; once you begin to engage with the crowd, you loosen up and they loosen up. Cast and audience are about to spend a few hours together sharing the space in a theatre. It would feel good to kick off that time by shaking out the nerves and settling in for a good time ahead.

At work: Why do we need it in the workplace?

How teams spend time before big moments at work never ceases to amaze me. And not always in a good way.

A big team moment could be the presentation of a significant deliverable or the pitch of a proposal to a group of decision-makers. The time spent right before those moments, those precious hours or minutes, are often directed towards non-essential activities and therefore completely wasted. Teams rarely warm up together and rarely work together to generate the collective and collaborative energy required for those big moments.

Let's walk through an example based on a compilation of real experiences. If you are in the workplace, working with teams and don't see yourself or anyone you know in this example in any way, please know how rare of a unicorn professional you are.

Example:
A team is brought together for a few weeks to create a business case (though this could be any work product for any purpose) for a new

initiative, which they want to mobilize and intend to take to a new stakeholder for approval. Members of the team are hand-picked from different functional areas, technical areas, and geographies to bring together the absolute best thinking. Weeks are comprised of spending time on conference calls, sharing materials online, and working through late nights. The business case is brilliant. The materials are brilliant.

Finally, the team, made up of individuals who have never been in the same physical room together, comes together on a Tuesday morning for a 9 a.m. presentation to the decision-making committee.

The team starts to arrive, one by one, assembling in the company's lobby. One by one they check in, show driver's licenses, and request Wi-Fi usernames and passwords. Why each team member needs Wi-Fi is uncertain, but nonetheless these requests draw out the check-in process by at least two to three minutes per person. The printer is down; the security officer checking in the team must ask another security desk to print the Wi-Fi passwords in a separate office. Finally, the Wi-Fi handouts are printed, delivered, and presented to each of the team members. The team then waits to be escorted to a conference room. The team then goes to the conference room, waiting outside the room while another group wraps up their meeting and exits, finally leaving the room available for the team to set up.

Once the team is in the conference room, each team member logs on to his and her own machines, testing the Wi-Fi passwords. Wi-Fi works for some, not others. For those experiencing issues with the Wi-Fi, a trip down to the security desk is required where the printing, delivering, and presentation of an updated Wi-Fi password takes place.

For those team members who did not experience an issue with the Wi-Fi password, they are opening emails and responding in some cases on topics that have nothing to do with the day's presentation at 9 a.m.; the presentation about which they should be focused. The presentation that should be solely in their thoughts in these moments right before the presentation itself and nothing else.

Who needs water? Who needs to go to the bathroom?

> *Is this a big pitch or a preschool class? Often, I personally have been the one in need of both water and the bathroom, so I'll allow this condescending question and judgment.*

The team is all together in the room, back from the break rooms and the bathrooms. Some have Wi-Fi; some gave up. Is it time to gel as a team? To get mentally, intellectually, and physically ready for the meeting, together, as a team?

No. No, it is not.

It has become the time when the team is looking through the materials to ensure there are page numbers on every page, the font is consistent, and the punctuation at the end of a list is consistent. Someone needs to check the connection to the videoconference line since some attendees will be remote and will need to log in and view the document online.

That's it. Time has run out. The stakeholders are entering the room — did anyone consider how to engage them properly before this big presentation to get them talking more comfortably? No. Well, now it's showtime!

I wish I could say that this illustrative example is the exception. I wish I could say that this is a rare case when a team happens to focus on all the wrong things instead of the right ones to become fully ready for a big meeting. I'd like to say those things. However, unfortunately I cannot say that since this illustrative example does in fact represent the norm.

I have spoken to numerous executives from a variety of companies and industries, each with similar stories and examples when they meet up as a team for a critical meeting or presentation. Colleagues show up in a room, as a collection of individuals. They fuss about logistical details before getting started. And yet we expect (every time) for the magic of clicking as a team and gelling as a cohort to just happen.

So, what's the gap? Intellectually, we agree that when we enter a meeting as a team for a common purpose, it is advantageous to behave as a cohesive team. We agree that a team's chemistry is an important factor when a stakeholder is deciding to invest in or work with a team or even trust a team to be able to deliver a certain outcome. We agree that we should support each other throughout the entire discussion with a common mantra: we're in this together. We agree that we should be pumped up with alert minds and bodies in order to respond to questions or topics unforeseen. We would agree on all of this. So, why are we focused on Wi-Fi, water, bathrooms, and punctuation during those final precious moments? Because we have not been trained in the workplace to behave any differently.

Until now.

Imagine if we showed up differently. Imagine if we were able to sync up and then show up connected as a team, assured that the magic will happen. The secret ingredient here is: prioritizing time for a team to warm up individually and together a team. Take that time. Write out a schedule for the team and include this warm-up time as you would the time needed for registration or technology set up. Set up your team for success as you would your Wi-Fi connection.

Activities: Get to work

The rule around warming up is simple… to practice warming up.

Warming up can fall into three categories in the workplace and can be accessed any time prior to stepping foot into the "spotlight," which I would define as any moment at work when you and your team are facilitating, demonstrating, presenting, collaborating, influencing, or discussing — basically whenever you and your team are speaking with others who are listening and speaking back to you.

- Warm up individually: Ensure that you're prepared for what's coming.
- Warm up as a team: Get ready mentally and physically, together.
- Warm up your stakeholders (around your team).

Let's get to work with these activities you can practice in any team meeting, because: (a) it's always a good idea to warm up a team; and (b) it's always good to practice these in the comfort of a team setting without the "spotlight" so that you can bring a strong level of confidence towards those times when you are prepping before a main event.

Activity 1A. Warm up individually: Centering oneself with vocal warm-ups.

Instructions:
1. Find a quiet place where you feel comfortable looking a little silly for a few minutes.
2. Make the sounds of each vowel, short and long sounds, by using as much of your mouth as possible — stretching your mouth as wide as you can.
3. Add the whole alphabet into your rotation if time allows.
4. For increased entertainment value, try doing this activity with your team either in unison or standing around in a circle with one person taking a vowel sound (aye), followed by the next person taking the next vowel sound (eee), and so on and so forth.
5. If doing this activity as a team and trying to make a good impression on a supervisor, stakeholder, or client, please consider NOT doing this warm-up in the receptionist lobby, office hallway, or parking lot to reduce the chance of an unwelcome audience forming.

Why do this:

- Takes your mind off any anxiety or unproductive nervous energy you might be storing.
- Loosens up your facial muscles allowing oxygenated blood into your face and brain (or so I think; I'm no face nor brain specialist).
- Minimizes the possibility of becoming tongue-tied by working out those verbal kinks in advance.

Activity 1B. Warm up individually: Being mindful of your goals.

Instructions:

1. In a quiet moment and before things get busy, grab a piece of paper and writing utensil.
2. Set an alarm for five to 10 minutes.
3. Write down the 10 messages or goals you have for this "spotlight" time, for you personally and for your team, holistically.
4. Try also practicing this activity as a team. Once each person writes down their messages or goals, share as a team to compare notes, ensure alignment, and enable the team to support one another's goals.

Why do this:

- Allows you to get in front of what's ahead of you.
- Increases the likelihood that you'll recall and then communicate what is most important to communicate and not get lost in some other details or others' agendas allowing you to be thoughtful, strategic, and proactive, as well as reactive.

Activity 1C. Warm up as a team: Creating and passing energy.

Instructions:

1. Stand in a circle with your team.

2. Alternate giving high and low fives as the energy moves around the circle.

3. For those ready for a more advanced warm-up, be creative! Try team jumping jacks, hum a song together, do simple arm raising stretches, or follow the leader around a room. Switch leaders every 10 steps to move in different directions. As long as everyone is having fun together and shaking out the nerves, you are doing this activity correctly.

4. Don't do anything too strenuous; no sense in a team member getting injured before entering into the spotlight. Also, per an aforementioned warning, please consider finding private space for this activity without an unwelcome set of passersby getting a little show, if putting on a show is not a desired outcome of this warm-up.

Why do this:
- Takes mind off anxiety and any potential nerves. You should see a pattern with these warm-ups.
- Allows for team connections and silly bonding across the team.
- Stretches muscles high and low.

Activity 1D. Warm up stakeholders: Opening topics.

Instructions:
1. Pair up to practice different types of warm-ups for a group of stakeholders.
2. In each pair, identify who will be Person A and who will be Person B.
3. Person A will identify a theme to kick off a presentation, such as: weekend activities, sports, weather, big global event, and initiate a discussion on that topic as though Person B were either one individual or a group of stakeholders.
4. Person B will respond to Person A's prompts and hold a brief dialogue (back and forth) for two minutes.

5. Switch roles so that Person B must identify a theme and initiate the discussion.

6. Debrief. How did it feel? Are there themes that Person A or Person B were more comfortable initiating?

> *In the real setting, you will want to consider the group dynamic. In some group settings, it will be sufficient to start the conversation with a simple, how is everyone doing today or a Happy Tuesday. These stakeholder warm-ups do not need to be lengthy, nor overly complicated to be effective.*

Why do this:

- Opens the conversation with a topic that is already thought through, which has a calming effect.
- Reminds everyone in the room subconsciously that the room is filled with people, just humans, no matter how lofty the main topic is that will be discussed later.

Activity 1E. Warm up your stakeholders: Ice breaker.

Instructions:

1. Before a team gets together, pick an ice breaker to kick things off; in other words, build the ice breaker into your meeting agenda.

2. Feel free to insert the ice breaker of your choosing, here's one to consider in your rotation, which is one of my favorites, particularly when I'm meeting a group of people for the first time: Ask the room to pick an activity on which they have some expertise and could give a "how-to" talk. For example, I might give a "how-to" talk on improv and not give one on how to play soccer well.

3. Note that they do not need to give the talk unless there is much more time to allow for this; they need only share the topic and perhaps some rationale as to why they picked that topic and why they have become experts.

Why do this:

- Allows folks to open up and start to discuss a topic with which they are already comfortable and have some knowledge, bringing confidence and comfort into the room.
- Allows you to get to know one another better and have topics about which to chat during the break.

Considerations

A steadfast consideration for warming up properly is to arrive on time, though I would advocate, get there *early*.

I have always been a fan of getting into the room where the big meeting will be conducted and settling in so that I can get as comfortable as possible in those surroundings — at least as much as my nerves will allow.

Sometimes the benefits of this early arrival extend beyond what could have been imagined.

Earlier in my career, I had the responsibility of facilitating a significant workshop with a group of senior industry leaders. Before the meeting time, I wanted to get comfortable in the room, practice standing at the front of the room, and even practice delivering some of the presentation. I also wanted to take some of that extra time to get to know others as they arrived.

As I was finishing up the set-up of the projector and the audio from my laptop, I noticed a very "Friendly Looking Person" who we will refer to as "FLP" for short. We started to chat about the Northeast traffic and the unseasonably warm weather in the area.

I then excused myself from our conversation as I became aware that I was in fact having trouble setting up the projector. My projector fix-it skills were, at that time, limited to unplugging the projector, plugging it in again, tapping the projector with increasing rigor until some rattling would suggest that either something was fixed, or things were made much worse. Imagine my surprise when those techniques alone did not seem to remedy the situation.

I applied all these limited Herculean tech skills. I unplugged it and plugged it back in. Turned it off and on. Turned it off and on. Turned it off and on. Tap, tap. Pressed all buttons, which has always been my last resort though it has never worked.

FLP must have seen my struggles and came back up to me and asked if I needed help. I weighed my options and quickly concluded that, yes, I needed help. FLP fiddled with the projector for a while, applying similar techniques as I had applied, and then offered to run down the hall and get a new one for the meeting. Very grateful, I thanked him and off he went.

About 10 seconds later, one of my more senior colleagues came up to me and asked what that was all about. What was I saying to FLP? What did FLP say to me? I remember being somewhat surprised by the questions. Could I not talk to a tech repair person about helping with a piece of tech without this inquisition? So, I told my colleague that things were "all good" and that I met the nice tech repair guy in the room, and he was running down the hall to get us a new projector.

He slowed down his speech and asked me again, "Who were you talking to?"

I repeated myself at an equally slow pace, "I was talking to the tech repair person, a really nice guy; he is going to get us a new projector for our meeting."

My colleague smiled and said, "I'm glad you got the chance to meet with the *Chief Information Officer*, who I'm sure is perfectly capable of running out and getting us some new office equipment."

Look, was I embarrassed a bit that I had skipped the step of introductions with FLP? Yes, yes, I was. However, I was grateful to have met FLP the way I did, comfortably, just two professionals engaging in discussion. Though I was initially caught off guard when it came to my attention how senior of a professional FLP was, when we started the meeting, the room most definitely was warmed up. People are people no matter how senior.

Warnings

Like all good things, you must be particularly careful with the stakeholder warm-up. I attempted to caveat this collective warm-up by saying you may need to adjust your approach based on several variables. I'll try to outline some reminders to help as you think through what adjustments are needed.

- Sometimes you will be expected to just start without much of a warm-up with your stakeholders. There might be limited time for you to make your points; you may only have a few minutes. Please adjust a warm-up expectation to your situation.
- Remember, you are not a professional stand-up comedian, so select your warm-up approaches carefully and respectfully — if you are a stand-up comedian outside of the workplace, unless there's a microphone in your hand and folks have drinks in their hands and you're in a comedy club, please consider *avoiding* the following opening remarks:
  - Raise your hand out there, how many of you flew in from out of state; aren't your arms tired?
    - Don't use this line.
    - This is just embarrassing.

- o Any new relationships in the room? Anyone want to find a new relationship in the room?
  - Don't use this line either.
  - This is a Human Resources nightmare.
- o Is it me, or is it just hot in here?
  - Oh no.
  - Human Resources nightmare again; there must be a better, more appropriate way to comment on the weather or lack of a fully functioning air conditioning system.
- Avoid poking the room with contentious topics in your warm-up. May I please steer you away from politics unless you are certain the room is aligned (i.e., you're leading a particular political party's working group meeting).

Reflections

At the end of each chapter with activities, take a few minutes, after you have practiced, and write down your thoughts.

You can either capture free-flowing thoughts on a separate piece of paper, digital notepad, or the lined text box provided here.

VI

THE BE CURIOUS RULE

Overview: What's the rule?

Unless you are truly omniscient (and if you are, you probably know what I'm going to say next), we are each best able to navigate and succeed at work when we recognize the importance and necessity of the knowledge that others possess. It is incredibly powerful and advantageous to understand what others have accomplished, where others have stumbled, how they have reached professional goals, and what they learned from failures or great wins. In order to harness the power of what others know, we must explore the art and science of being curious and sharpen the skill of asking questions. In this section we'll explore the power of questions reminding us of two key facts: 1) alone we do not have all the answers; and 2) we are only able to unleash the power of asking questions, when those from whom we are seeking answers are valued and appreciated for sharing that information with us.

In improv: How does it work in improv comedy?

When two actors are creating a scene together, asking questions of one another is a powerful tool. It serves as a method to discover new information, to allow each to shape ideas and potentially to bring others onto the stage. How so? The following questions are examples of how to achieve those objectives on stage.

- "Why do you always insist on wearing slippers when we go to the movies?"
  - ○ Purpose: Gives the respondent some direction on what to share next.
- "How was your trip to the moon last week?"
  - ○ Purpose: Gives the respondent some history with which to now create some interesting stories.
- "Do you hear something over there that sounded eerily like either screeching racecar tires or your mother-in-law?"
  - ○ Purpose: Gives another actor backstage a possible part in the scene to enter, either as a rushed racecar driver or the mother-in-law herself.

These questions are like gifts on stage. Some direction will surface that previously did not exist in the conversation only moments ago.

For the one asking the questions, the opportunity exists to be generous and to tee up a question rather than taking the punchline for themselves directly. The punchline doesn't need to be one for the taking each time. If done properly, an actor can set up another actor for the starring funny line with well-placed questions.

An audience senses when a cast member is setting up one another for success, rather than watching a particular actor go for all the glory (a.k.a. the punchline) all the time.

It's clear that asking questions of another actor is a fantastic way to get a conversation going or keep the scene moving along, and it can also support someone who might be stuck and help uncover new ways to explore a scene. There are times when it becomes easy to get stressed on stage, to feel worried and panicked that a scene is flailing and not coming together in a way where a resolution is in sight, plus an audience may not be laughing. The horror! When that panic pops up, asking a question is a collaborative approach to work together in those moments with some small prompts to get the momentum moving again, *together*.

At work: Why do we need it in the workplace?

One of the most prominent issues in the workplace is poor decision making, which stems from not having enough information to properly guide decisions, whether those decisions are being made for a business, an employee individually, or to promote a more inclusive work environment broadly. Let's explore each of these cases.

Business decision: Look before you leap (to answers).

When I started my consulting career, I thought the expectation was — you ask me a question, and I answer, something like:

- You ask a question, I answer.
- You ask another question, I answer.
- And so on, and so forth. See the pattern?

Quickly you realize that in the business world, there are times when you might be asked a question yet might need more information to serve the question well. In other words, you might need to ask more questions to understand the background and the issue versus jumping into problem-solving mode without enough information.

For example, I am often asked to give a recommendation based on industry trends or based on the broader business landscape. There was a time in my career when I would just blurt out these recommendations as requested. Respecting what is required to answer diligently, I now approach these requests differently with the necessary reflection, and in most cases, respond with my own request for information, so that I can contribute more insightful recommendations. These days I might say something like this:

- "Before I share my thoughts on what's right for your specific organization, I have a few questions for you that will help me customize that thinking."
- "Let me start by sharing some broad trends; for a recommendation, let's talk about what's first most important here and what you want for this organization."

Logically, this sounds very, well, *logical*. Of course, you would want to hold back an opinion on something if you don't have all the information.

However, I watch this trap set all the time, and I watch very smart people fall into the trap most of the time. Why?

Typically, it is because we want to help one another.

This desire to help people isn't a bad thing. In fact, said positively, this is a *great* thing. It's simply that we may do each other harm when we try to answer something without enough information.

What can happen when we jump to an answer or solution without a much-needed pause?

Imagine a friend standing in a restroom that is flooding. In his state of panic, he asks you if you can go out and bring him a pair of rain boots.

You can certainly rise to the occasion and say, "Yes, of course!" And proceed to solve for the rainboots — ankle height or to the knee, yellow or red, maybe glow in the dark or a special design.

However, another approach might be to respond with a question: "How can we turn off the water?"

It is possible that footwear was not the best way to tackle the circumstances surrounding you and your friend. By asking some follow-up questions, you both might be able to resolve the situation faster and find yourselves in a less urgent state sooner.

It is important to remind yourself to ask questions, be curious, and learn. So, when you do respond with a perspective, recommendation, or solution, those are built on a thoughtful and firm foundation.

Employee decision: Listen/coach versus tell.

I've had the great honor of coaching people in their careers and have been coached by some of the best.

It wasn't until I studied what it means to be a coach that I realized that I don't do it well all the time. I jump into fix-it mode too quickly as so many of us do. Why?

Again, typically it is because we want to help each other.

When most people hear even a glimmer that something is bothering another individual in their lives, they want to fix it — I certainly do. I do it at work; I do this at home; I can't help myself.

- *Kids fighting over something.*
- *Easy, you think.*
- *Give the thing back to its rightful owner and apologize, you say.*
- *Make them hug.*
- *Rinse and repeat.*

But it's rarely that simple, certainly not that simple when the two kids in question aren't toddlers anymore, have feelings and thoughts of their own, and they are fighting over a concept, not an object.

At work, it might come in the guise of someone who is simply unhappy with the current role, current supervisor, or current working environment. When you attempt to throw out solutions, you might completely miss the underlying issue.

Though true, we are still constantly in conversations giving each other advice when we might not have all the information to give the best advice.

Whether you are a career coach, advisor, mentor, or you work with one, think about how many questions are asked before advice is shared.

- Are the full set of circumstances around a problem understood?
- Are thoughts and feelings understood?
- Before advice is to be dispensed, does the dispenser try to get the person to articulate what advice they would give themselves?
- How often do we say, "What do you think you could have done differently? What can you do to change how this is going now, having more knowledge now than you had before? A year from now, what would you like to be able to say about how you made this better, easier, or more inspiring?"
- Rather, how often do we say, "Here's what I would do…" or "Here's what I've done in a similar situation…" or worse "Do this…?"

Consider how might you apply your own curiosity and set of questions to be better for your team members, colleagues, family, or friends.

Inclusive: All voices in the room.

Asking questions enables you to share the room with others. Obvious.

However, these rooms often include different voices, as well as different personalities with different experiences coming together. Some personalities are big, loud, and opinionated. Some personalities are more reserved, pensive, and analytical. Some experiences have taught people to share ideas of any range. Some experiences may have taught others to be selective in what is shared since ideas may be unwelcomed and judged harshly, a lesson perhaps learned when an individual interacted with a Lid.

Questions have the power to open the room to all types of individuals. A question can focus someone whose thoughts are scattered. A question can bring someone into the conversation who has gone quiet or didn't feel like they were senior enough to contribute. A question even has the power to engage participants around physical and virtual spaces, enabling participants to navigate the hybrid working environment more successfully.

Since we are increasingly working in hybrid work environments where some team members may be seated together around a physical table with others dialing in through a conference call or videoconference, it becomes even more important to ensure that those in a discussion, no matter where they sit, are able and comfortable to contribute.

Imagine being in a discussion you joined over the phone or videoconference while others are sitting around a physical table brainstorming a new product concept. They are lively as they speak, interrupt each other in a friendly way with their back and forth, yet you find it difficult to hear everyone (because of the overlapping conversations) and undoubtedly find it difficult to get a word into the conversation. You hang up after 60 minutes feeling more disconnected from the team and product vision than before the call started.

However, imagine now a different scenario in which several team members in the room recognized the need to pause their in-person discussion periodically with a question for those participating via phone or videoconference to ensure that all joining electronically were able to contribute just as effectively. They might say something like, "Let's pause for a moment and make sure we're not dominating the conversation here. Would anyone who is joining remotely want to share their thoughts?" How inclusive, respectful, and engaged could the discussion become by taking the time to ask a question and bring the rest of the virtual team along on the team's journey." Take the time to be curious and formulate questions. Use questions as a means to get smarter regarding a subject or situation. Use questions as a means to engage the world around you.

Showing up with questions is powerful: use this power wisely and often.

Activities: Get to work.

How can we practice the art of asking questions? How can we create an activity aimed at reminding everyone to ask additional questions? Simple. We'll explore the art of asking questions in an activity that is made up of… only asking questions. That's crazy, you say. Let's give it a try.

Worth noting, this is an activity that you can practice most places with the right set up. You can bring this activity into your team at the start of a team meeting or the day before a new customer or stakeholder introduction meeting. You could even practice this activity with family and friends, getting together during a holiday or just over a simple meal. I have practiced this one with my own kids while driving them to and from school or weekend activities; in that setting the key is getting them to eventually answer a question.

This activity is a fun and quick reminder that it is okay to not jump on a topic, yet rather invite others to share their thoughts.

Then you collectively can take stock of the best way to move forward in discussion or action. Does jumping forward still make sense? Or does a smaller more calculated next step make better sense?

Activity 2A. Questions Game in Pairs.

Instructions:
1. Break into pairs.
   a. A team of three will work just as well, especially if your group has an uneven number of participants — this flexibility prevents excluding anyone from the exercise.
2. Agree on a relationship for the pairs or a location in which the conversation will take place.
   a. Examples of relationships for the pairs might include: siblings, teachers, students, job interviewees, interviewers, or you can get creative to customize a relationship of your own.
   b. Examples of locations might include: grocery store, train station, breakroom at work, another planet, or again, get creative with a location of your choice.
3. Determine who will go first.
4. Begin a conversation with the rule that each person is only allowed to ask a question back (not answer the question asked of them).
   a. If this rule is broken (i.e., someone responds with a statement not a question), please simply acknowledge, take a pause, and continue the dialogue again with one of the members of the pair asking a question to get back into the flow of the activity.
5. End after two minutes.

When I've run this activity in workshops, I typically show the group what it sounds like for a few rounds, so here's an example between this pair, Person One and Person Two:
- Person One: "How are you doing?"
- Person Two: "How do you think I'm doing?"

Repeating the same question in this game is a bit of a cheat response. I typically let a participant get away with a limited number of cheats when I'm around and simply ask them to try to apply a bit more creativity to their questions so the interaction can advance. I ask them to do this as I'm smiling so the person typically receives the feedback positively.

- Person One: "What were you thinking when you came to work in full kangaroo costume?"
- Person Two: "Aren't we very heads down here, focused on work, and need a laugh?"
- Person One: "Why kangaroo?"
- Person Two: "Why not?"
- Scene (i.e., End of this example)

Activity 2B. Questions Game for a Group.

Instructions:
1. Preferably this activity follows Activity 2A, in which individuals can warm up with the questions game in pairs.
2. Identify four individuals to go in front of the rest of the group.
3. Identify two individuals to go to centerstage, with a person off to the right side and another person off to the left side, in queue, in the wings, or waiting for their turn to come up to centerstage at the right time.
4. Agree on a relationship or location for the pair on centerstage.
5. The pair then initiates a conversation using only questions as they go back and forth.
6. When one of them is unable to reply quickly with a question (i.e., the pause is too long) or responds in a statement rather than a question, that person is tapped out by the person standing on their side of the space (the one in the queue) and that new person now enters the scene. Onto centerstage, front of the room.

7. One of the original members of the pair now remains centerstage joined by this new individual, and they continue the discussion with only questions.

8. Each time an individual is unable to respond back in the form of a question, that individual is tapped out by the individual waiting on their side of the wings until a two-minute time-period comes to an end.

Why do this:

- Reminds your psyche of the power of questions.
- Reminds your psyche that you do not always need to respond to a question if it's best to collect more information.
- Reminds your psyche that you should consider how to use questions to engage others in a discussion rather than talk *at* people.

Now take some time to debrief from the activity as a group. Was it easy or hard? Did you find yourself starting to answer the question versus ask another question during the exercise? Did you find the exercise gets easier with time?

Considerations

For the most part, I've watched people struggle at first with this exercise, who have been programmed to answer and solve immediately. It can be uncomfortable to be asked a question and not quiet the voice in your head that wants you to answer to please people and do that which you believe is expected.

It's worth considering, this activity is not meant to teach you to always ask questions; we'll get to more detail on that in the Warnings section. Rather, it is meant to consciously remind you of the power of questions and at least to ask yourself if your best course of action, when you are asked a question, is to answer that question or instead to seek out additional information. Being aware of when to answer and when to ask follow-up questions, when you lack sufficient information to answer well, is more than half the battle.

I would also ask you to consider the power of questions when you are checking in on your own team — and consider when one question alone may not be enough, so preparation of follow-up questions may be needed.

What does that mean, you might ask?

I reflect on how often in a workday we overuse the question, "How are you?" And how often we are satisfied with someone's answer of, "Fine" and then move on to the work agenda prepared. Is it possible that we should consider asking a few more questions in different ways to understand truly how our teammates and colleagues are really doing?

A few follow-up questions may help us provide better support to each other in the workplace and as humans. Following an initial, "How are you?" and "Fine," some questions to consider as you aim to care for the people around you include:

- Anything you'd change about the week we just had?
- Anything keeping you up at night?
- If I told you I could take one thing off your plate right now (not saying I can yet), what would that be?
- Anything we can do so that you could answer the "How are you" question with "Excellent" instead of just "Fine"?

This list is obviously intended to be inspiring and not exhaustive. The point is that the power of questions can be applied in many ways and at varying levels in the workplace, including down to the very personal level of understanding how our teammates are doing. Just as we aim to understand a complex work issue, let's say, in the manufacturing space, it may take more than one question to understand exactly what is going on with an individual, why there seems to be an issue, and how we might work together to address that issue.

Warnings

This activity comes with a few warnings, which I'm sure those around you would appreciate that we address.

Please remember two things:

- This is an exercise. It is a game, an activity; please do not necessarily subject others in your daily life to this back-and-forth banter in normal conversation. You may risk others being annoyed, frustrated, or overall unhappy with your discussion tactics.

- Related to the point above, sometimes you are asked a question, and you should just answer the question. The question requires an answer that should squarely be in your area of expertise, or you already have completed the data gathering required to go ahead and answer the question. That's right, there are times when you might just have all the information needed to go ahead and *answer*. For example, I recently took a flight for a work meeting. If I was asked by someone, "Was it on time?" I'd probably just go ahead and answer; it either was on time or it wasn't on time. No sense in drawing out that part of the conversation by peppering in further clarifying questions before you answer, "Well, why do you ask? What do you mean by that? Do you ask that question of everyone you meet who just took a flight?" Answer the question and move on.

Being curious improves the decision-making process, as well as the result and does not mean that teams should become paralyzed in that decision-making process altogether. It means that there are times when we could all benefit from knowing more before we jump to a solution or a conclusion. We also should recognize that sometimes we need to ask questions in order to engage people in a discussion or bring out the best thinking from people in the room who might just need that extra inquiry for brilliance to emerge. Take the time to explore how, when, and where to bring questions more into the workplace. Why not? You must have known I'd end this section with a question, right?

Reflections

At the end of each chapter with activities, take a few minutes, after you have practiced, and write down your thoughts.

You can either capture free-flowing thoughts on a separate piece of paper, digital notepad, or the lined text box provided here.

VII

THE TELL YOUR STORIES RULE

Overview: What's the rule?

In short, this rule requires some reflection and homework: know your stories so you can tell them. The rule is to think back over your life, experiences, and identify stories that stand out to you. The standing out part could be for a variety of reasons, which we'll get back to in a moment. Keep an inventory of your good stories, the meaningful ones, the funny ones, and the insightful ones. Jot down a few sentences about the story so you can recall details when you choose to share those details with others.

What is a standout story? How do we identify which of our stories we should put on a list?

A standout story may be on your list because you learned something from an experience found in that story or you took away a life lesson that helped shape who you are today, or why you make certain life choices. A standout story may also find its way to your story list because it was just plain funny. Hilarious. Fall-down laughing *hilarious*. It might have been that funny because of something someone said to you, something you said, or just a turn of events. Either way, telling that story to someone else may bring them the same amount of laughter burst that it brought you. Perhaps the story was the opposite of funny; it was more melancholic and therefore may be an empathy-evoking story. The reasons may differ as to why a story would be on your list of stories to remember, but the one thing all the stories should have in common: they're memorable and worth telling again.

In improv: How does it work in improv comedy?

In improv comedy, which by nature isn't scripted, knowing your stories has benefits.

For one, knowing your stories, which include characters with unique attributes, can inspire you to recall those attributes when shaping new and interesting characters for a scene. And you never know when one interesting detail about a person from your past may help you find an interesting path in a scene or get a laugh.

For example, I was able to pull a characteristic from a childhood story, about a friend with a unique personal passion around food coverings for the microwave. This childhood story involved a friend of mine who was so relaxed about everything in her house. We could eat in the family room, stay up late, watch TV, or play video games with no time limits. But, if I tried, even attempted, to heat something up in the microwave without a paper towel on top, the wrath of fire came out. I only made that mistake once. Okay, I was 13 so I made that mistake a few times, but then I stopped making that mistake. Out of that experience and story, I would later introduce a crazy paper towel lady character into a scene.

Another source of character inspiration came from another childhood story that took place around the time that Michael Jackson's *Thriller* music video was popular. The music video was amazing. A theatrical masterpiece. The music, the dancing, and the zombies. While dancing around the room with my sister at her friend's house, my sister's hair got caught in the fan. At the time, the technology did not exist to pause live television, take care of something, and then return to the program, like you can do today. Oh no. If you turned your attention away from something on the tv, you missed it. And we had waited a long time for this particular music video to air on MTV. So, when her hair got caught in the fan, any other child with friends would have turned their attention to the hair caught in the fan and helped get the hair out of the fan. Not us. We did unplug the fan, yes. But then we finished watching the *Thriller* video *first* before addressing the actual hair in the fan issue. Yes, my sister's dancing abilities were more constrained as she became less mobile than she had been before the hair-fan incident. We would eventually call a parent into the room to help after Vincent Price started his spooky laughter at the end of the video. The hair was fully salvaged. But who does that? So, a new characteristic emerged, one of an individual who must finish what is front of her despite finding herself in some precarious situations. I would later find a home for that characteristic in an improv scene.

The nice thing about improv and theatre in general is that you do not need to be true to a real story or a real character when on stage. However, when your stories, various characters, and experiences are closer to the surface of your brain, it is much easier to be inspired by them and have the flexibility to bring them into what's happening on stage.

At work: Why do we need it in the workplace?

Knowing your stories is a powerful tool in general. There is plenty of information out there that explains the power of storytelling. Stories connect us to our pasts, connect us to each other, help us understand one another, and explain why we behave the way we do.

In the workplace, if you can think about when the lessons or themes in your stories might be relevant to a current situation or theme, your stories have an ability to make the points come to life that you would like to make. They can make a case for change, make a business proposal come to life, and make for more pleasant brainstorming sessions.

Take the great topic of predicting technology trends effectively and the skill and art it takes for professionals to determine those trends.

A few years ago, I started a discussion on the following topic with colleagues: how difficult it is to predict which technology trends will stick (think: cell phones) versus not stick (think: VHS and Beta). Some generations may need to search those terms; I'm certain I have a few of those historical artifacts in my basement for those interested. This topic then transitioned into a conversation about what game-changing technology means, recognizing that sometimes a game changer is not initially welcomed with open arms.

To enrich this topic, I shared such a story, where I found myself to be initially an anti-game changer.

My personal story on… getting a tech trend wrong

When I was a senior in high school, I saw a few of my older friends leave for college, but with tears in my eyes, I remained hopeful that we'd remain in contact by exchanging letters and talking occasionally. Then one day one of those friends sent me an electronic mail message, which I was somehow able to open in the computer lab at my school.

What is this? A message from a friend coming through a computer?!

This electronic exchange of messages will never stick, I thought. No one will want to communicate this way. People prefer to write and receive real letters. People take great joy out of seeing something personally for them when they go to the mailbox. Woo-hoo, they would think or say. They got a letter. They would open the envelope with great anticipation, they would pull out the piece of paper, unfold that piece of paper, and then, oh happy day! They would read their friend's handwriting, wishing them well or explaining a recent event.

The art of real mail writing, receiving, and reading is a beautiful thing. This digital, electronic mail thing will undeniably flop, I thought. I assured myself that I would never fall into this electronic mail trap. I am a real letter writer. That's me. There's history in that. There's beauty in that. Our ability to handwrite thoughts is part of what makes us human. I will never turn to this electronic mail shortcut of communication. So, I replied to my friend the only way I knew how: a genuine handwritten letter.

Did I get that right? Did this electronic email thing flop? *Undeniably* it did not.

I like to think that I get some tech trends right, but clearly not email.

> *I may get some trends right, but worth noting, I also didn't get Netflix right. I thought, "Who doesn't like walking the aisles at a local Blockbuster to find a movie for the night?" We'll always want to do that. I also questioned shopping online. "How can you buy a shirt or shoes from a website without trying it on first? That's craziness."*

Two more personal stories: inventions and value

I decided to add these stories to my story list after thinking about how easy it is to claim you invented something that already had been invented.

I was (only partially) joking with a friend recently about how I basically invented the concept of storage bins and organizers before those became really popular (you're welcome, The Container Store though, no, I will not be making a legitimate claim to this effect). Growing up, I loved organization so much that I would collect shoe boxes and organize things in them, write a label on the front, and stack them on the shelves in my closet. I even had a box labeled, "small boxes." Yes, that's right, I stored small storage boxes in an only slightly bigger storage box. Clearly, I was the originator of the storage box empire. I never looked to see exactly when storage bins or boxes were marketed (could it have been, in fact, before I was even born), but as the saying goes, we won't let the facts get in the way of a good story.

Along this same theme of self-proclaimed inventors of things that would become very popular with no inventor recognition, I recalled another childhood story about all-you-can-eat buffets. The main story is that my mom once told me that she invented buffets. She has no data to support this claim, nor do I unfortunately. It is fun to imagine, though, what life could have been for my family and me if we were, in fact, the first family of the buffets.

However, we did enjoy a good buffet growing up.

This topic leads me to a secondary story around my mother, childhood buffet experiences, and the mother-daughter arguments that buffets would cause. At buffets I would go up to the various stations and fill up my plate with the least expensive items on the buffet which seemed to upset her. My plate would include two cups of plain lettuce and then about one to two tablespoons of Ranch dressing, sometimes I'd add a spoonful of broccoli, if feeling so inclined. Then I'd have two small side dishes, one of mashed potatoes, and one of corn. My mother would ask me to go up and get more food or ask if I could get something with beef. She would say, "Let's get our money's worth." I resisted. I wanted my lettuce, Ranch, potatoes, and corn. At some point, I came up with this wise response, "Why do we want to pay for a stomach ache?" Then eventually as I got older, these even wiser words were hatched, "Isn't it worth the money if I enjoy what I eat and don't overeat?"

I recall and recant this story when engaging in discussions today about the value of money, perceived versus realized, paying for what you *value* versus paying for what is *of value* to others.

Our messages are much more powerful and memorable when we bring stories into the discussion as well. In the "Be Curious" chapter, I told the story of the bathroom flooding and the request for boots to make the point about the importance of asking questions. What are your stories and for what purposes?

Without these stories, we're really just walking fortune cookie fortunes. Know your stories and the reason each story may be relevant to the person with whom you're engaging and the points you aim to make.

Activities: Get to work

Time to sharpen your minds and think about your stories. This activity challenges you to: (1) know your stories, the meaningful ones; and (2) get comfortable sharing concisely. The exercise of knowing your stories is only halfway; for your stories and lessons to be of use to someone in the workplace or anywhere for that matter, you must practice sharing them in a way that people can hear you, hold attention, and therefore connect to your messages.

Activity 3A. Share a story with a person.

Instructions:
1. Each person individually.
   a. Take two to three minutes to write down a list of two to three meaningful stories from your life with enough words that you'll remember the story later in the exercise. What makes a story meaningful? Here are a few prompts:

     i.   An experience and story that shaped a life lesson by which you now live, think about often, and even share with others in some form.

    ii. A story in which you were the observer but learned something that would stick with you and shape how you act, treat people, take care of yourself, or set personal or professional priorities.

  b. Review your list and pick one that you would be comfortable sharing with a partner and potentially the team.

2. Take turns sharing your stories in pairs.

  a. Person A takes two to three minutes to share a personal story, ending with the life lesson and why that is an important lesson for the individual, perhaps including how the lessons could be applied today.

  b. Person B shares feedback on the story, perhaps sharing how it relates to their own life, or could be applied.

  c. It is now Person B's turn to share their story.

  d. Person A now gives feedback.

Why do this:

- Get comfortable recalling stories from your own life, stories from others that you have heard, stories in general that you think have meaning, were of benefit to you, and therefore may be of benefit to others.

- Get comfortable sharing your stories briefly to hold the attention of others.

- Beyond this activity, consider in which situations you may find that story, its lessons, or its meaning beneficial to others in the workplace.

Activity 3B. Share a story with a broader audience.

Instructions:

1. Following the exercise in pairs, consider asking two to three people to share their stories with the broader group or the whole team.

2. Those individuals will then share their stories, which they first shared within their pair.

3. Debrief together with the following types of questions:

    a. How did it feel to generate the list of stories at the beginning? Are there more stories that you could and would have written down if you had more time?

    b. When will you make that time to continue to write your list of meaningful events or experiences that could create great storytelling?

    c. How did it feel to tell your story? Were you comfortable? If you weren't, why do you think you weren't? How could you have been more comfortable, if you had more time or less time to share? What about if you had more time to think about the details of your story? When will you find that time?

    d. Who in your life is a great storyteller? Why do you think that is? How could you learn from that person?

Why do this:

- Take advantage of this opportunity to practice sharing one of your stories with an even broader audience.

- Seek feedback on the story, your delivery, and how it may or may not have been relevant to that particular group.

- As was said before, get comfortable telling your stories and your lessons in a practice setting so those stories and lessons are easier for you to recall in the real-world setting.

Considerations

Consider the workplace situations in which you are finding yourself:

- Are you building a new team?

- Are you creating a new strategy?

- Are you executing a strategy that already was defined?

- Is your department just trying to stay afloat with an increased workload?

- Are you flourishing at work, but forgetting to take care of your work-life balance?

Depending on your current situation it may be that you have a story or know of a story that may be relevant and of value to your team or colleagues around you. It may be that you have a story about a time when you spoke up to challenge thinking and it ended well or didn't end well because you faced some Lid behaviors, but the experience gave you clarity on the type of leader you want to be in the future. Or, perhaps your team is working too much, and you share a story that you read about someone who has taken back Wednesdays from the marathon of videocalls and works all day in exercise clothes, so that at 5 p.m., they are more likely to workout.

Whatever the situation may be, reflect on your life and consider which lessons and which stories should be brought more into the spotlight. Which of your stories, or those which you have adopted as your own, may inspire your colleagues? Which of your stories may simply help you relate to the situation? Show you're human, too? Let someone know that they are not alone with a struggle or challenge. Maybe you've been in a similar situation and found your way out — maybe you've been in a similar situation and floundered around only to find a coping mechanism in that floundering that they may find is helpful.

Consider proactively and preemptively how these stories, which have been stored in the depths of your psyche, may be brought closer to the surface of your brain and recalled more easily in the workplace when you need to share them with the people who need to hear them.

Warnings

Serious warning ahead. This rule is intended to get you thinking about your stories, how you might share with others in a variety of settings to be informative, interesting, entertaining (perhaps), and propel the discussion. It is also intended to make people comfortable sharing their stories.

It is not intended for you to go on and on about your life with no rhyme or reason. It is not intended for you to bore, overly preach, or otherwise unnecessarily annoy your colleagues, friends, nor family. One of my favorite expressions of recent is to "read the room." And, yes, this goes for the virtual room as well. Ask yourself, is this a good time for this story? Does it fit into the flow of the conversation? Is it the right time to talk about something that happened to me or does someone else have the floor or the attention right now, so it's not the right time to divert attention away? If you've already started the story, is it time to wrap it up? Has the group heard enough, got the point, and it's time to move on?

> *For those of you unfamiliar with the expression, "Read the room," I highly encourage further exploration. Sometimes a brilliant statement or funny line is not welcomed the way it could be if it were only offered in another moment of time. If the room doesn't seem ready or open to what you have to say, consider holding it back. Just because you want to say something doesn't mean that thing is ready to be heard.*

Storytelling is a phenomenal way to connect us to one another, but it can also create a wedge if you tell a story from a high horse. Is there a hero in all your stories — and is that hero always you? Do you come across too perfect, too enlightened, or too fantastical? Have you led someone to disconnect from the content of your story since it sounds too unrelatable, not relevant, or never-ending?

Be thoughtful with your stories, be concise, get to your point, and invite others to share as well. Be human. Use the stories to make connections, support each other. Be aware and advised, others have stories, too. Encourage others to share, enlighten, and connect. In this way, storytelling is a means to create bridges with each other and learn from one another. Storytelling allows us to share, understand, respect, and learn from each other's journeys with our interest and attention.

Reflections

At the end of each chapter with activities, take a few minutes, after you have practiced, and write down your thoughts.

You can either capture free-flowing thoughts on a separate piece of paper, digital notepad, or the lined text box provided here.

VIII

THE OPEN YOUR MIND RULE

Overview: What's the rule?

Congratulations, you made it to the quintessential rule of improv. The backbone around which most scene work is built. The backbone around which most good ideas (business or otherwise) develop. This rule has many names. You may know it is as the "Yes, and" rule and if that is the case I would say, "Yes, and" let's further discuss it.

This rule is one of my favorites, and it can be used anywhere: at work, at home, as well as anywhere you're speaking with another person and care about that person's contribution to the discussion or relationship.

It's the "Broaden your outlook," "Build upon ideas," "Anything can be possible" rule!

When a comment is shared by someone, this rule would suggest that you then pause and consider how you might support that comment on a journey. The rule would ask you to ask yourself, "How might you both explore this comment further versus shutting it down immediately?"

Make sense? "Yes, and" — let's *continue* to discuss further. We're just getting started.

In improv: How does it work in improv comedy?

In improvisational comedy, the application of being open to other actors' choices in a scene is one of the fundamental building blocks to a successful exchange of ideas and journey through a scene.

This may sound obvious to you.

Approaching an exchange of ideas with an open mind, as open as possible, gives those ideas the best opportunity to approach the impossible.

This openness requires a certain sense of risk taking, even optimism, by removing the conscious choice to negate, revert, or stop idea generation and flow just because you may not know exactly where that idea could go. In those moments where chances are taken and there is proof that new, out-there ideas can be good ones, confidence builds, and trust grows.

Let's break down an improv scene.

At the start of a scene, actors may only be given a location, relationship, or even just a first word. Then it's on. The scene is a go.

How will these actors create an experience on stage worthy of an audience's attention? Worthy of laughter? Why are they even around each other in that specific location? What makes the relationship between the characters, which the actors will portray, interesting enough — what will they do? What must they go through or avoid together? Who will take on which personality type? What conflict will be resolved and how?

If the actors approach their scene with rigidity and doubt, the scene is likely to fail. Typically, this failure is due to the team's lack of cohesion, they are not coming together in meaningful ways to create a story and then for that story to reach some sort of conclusion.

What might be happening?

They may not be taking subtle directional cues from one another to help the scene progress, so they are unable to build off what each is saying or doing successfully. They may be stopping each other from progressing the scene by dismissing or fully killing ideas presented by others. Therefore, they are not on a path together and that leaves the actors unaware of where to go in the scene. The inflexibility of the performers causes hostility on the stage, which is easily detected by the audience. This is very awkward for everyone involved.

Let's look at an actual improv example from my past. I once found myself in a scene with an actor where we were only given a location: a Chicago "L" stop, which is an elevated train station stop. Since I was performing improv comedy in and around Chicago at the time, it was a common location shouted out from the audience.

> *It still is unclear to me why so many people find this train platform such a humorous place to have conversations, but we were obliged to take this suggestion, especially if the suggestion was made loud enough such that it would be obvious if we chose to ignore it.*

So, there we were given the "L" stop. I remember turning to the actor next to me and saying, "Grandpa?"

My fellow actor went with it, put himself into that role, and we carried on. But what if that wasn't what happened. What if he stopped that choice?

Imagine a scenario in which the actor negated that relationship choice. Imagine how or if the scene would progress at all. How might the discussion feel to experience or watch with a conflict at the level of: how the characters relate to each other? What would happen next in the scenario in which the actor said, "I'm not your grandpa; I don't know who you are."

I can tell you as an actor I would have felt a variety of emotions and thought of a few names to call that fellow actor (in my head), but I digress. One emotion I would have felt would have been irritation. I would have been irritated. I took a risk in the scene and gave him the start of an identity, a "Grandpa," believing that the person up there on stage with me would build upon that choice and take the scene along its journey. I would then in turn continue to build upon his choices. In this scenario where he negated the relationship, the road to collaboration, as well as through the scene, just got a bit bumpier.

In improv, "yes, and" doesn't mean you must take each idea necessarily as the person intended to offer it in a predictable way. *What do I mean?*

Let's use the "Grandpa" example. Maybe you don't want to play the part of the grandpa, and that's okay. There are still ways to "yes, and" that idea and take it in a different direction.

After hearing yourself called "Grandpa," maybe you say, "Yes, I played the part of your grandpa years ago in the off-off-Broadway version of *The Princess Bride*, and we had a few nice scenes together, kid, but it's time to move on with your life. I'm on my way to an audition, care to join me?"

True, this "yes, and" didn't go quite where the scene may have gone with a simple grandpa/grandkid relationship queued up, but there was now so much more unexpected fun to be had on stage.

At work: Why do we need it in the workplace?

It is critical to be open to new ideas, to one another, and to the possibility that greatness can come from anyone at any time in the workplace. To be open to those new ideas, it is even more critical that people in the workplace are comfortable and confident to share those ideas.

There is much agreement in the workplace that the inclusion and diversity of people is necessary for healthy, thriving, forward-thinking businesses. I would add a critical ingredient. You may bring diversity into a workplace, but unless that diversity is truly embraced at the discussion level, meaning in conversations, the goal of that diversity cannot be achieved.

So, let's walk the talk. "Yes, and."

An open mindset allows us to demonstrate respect for diversity of people and draw out unique perspectives (different from your own). When an individual shares a new idea or a few sentences on a new idea, this is the time when "yes, and" can do its greatest magic. I like to call these newly formed ideas, baby ideas or "idea-lets" (like a piglet, but for an idea).

What happens when you close your mind off — say no — to other people's suggestions too soon, without hearing out the full idea-let?

In addition to depriving the universe of an idea-let such that the idea-let will never grow into its full potential as a fully functioning idea, you may shut down that individual from contributing much more — in that moment or forever with you. This is where you must be careful of your own Lid behavior.

Are you someone who shuts down baby ideas, idea-lets? Have you seen someone shut down idea-lets prematurely?

In a brainstorm, have you said any of these comments or have you heard them said by others when an idea-let has been shared:

- You missed the point.
- That's not it at all.
- That's not going to work here.
- That can't work here.
- We tried it before. It didn't work a few years ago.
- That may have been the dumbest idea I've ever heard.

Take this example, based on a true story. A team was brainstorming how to approach a certain deliverable, in this case a work product for a leadership team. The team members started to write ideas on a whiteboard, one by one.

The first team member mentioned their idea and then wrote it on the board; there were a few questions about the idea, more clarifying questions, and then the group moved on. The second team member had a similar experience. The brainstorming was going very well; people seemed relaxed about sharing their ideas.

However, then this happened. The next team member, one of the more junior team members, stood up and headed to the whiteboard to talk through an idea. A more senior team member read the idea-let and said, "You missed the boat; that's not it at all."

The room went silent. Absolutely silent.

That more senior team member then asked the team, "Any other *brilliant* ideas" to break loose from the silence, but the room did not recover. No other new idea was shared. The team stared at the list of two ideas on the whiteboard before asking a few more clarifying questions, then the team wrapped up and ended the meeting early. The room *never* recovered.

These negative responses not only impacted the individual who specifically shared the idea-let, but also impacted how and/or if others would share in the future. As we explored earlier, negative energy is highly contagious.

Whereas, when an idea-let is welcomed and embraced into the universe with curiosity and a "yes-and" mentality, the results can be far more encouraging. The idea-let is then given time to grow, or a better idea can emerge while the group learns more about the idea-let or learns more about what's most important to the team when they evaluate ideas in general. What's most important is that when the team continues to promote and recognize those participating, communicating, and collaborating, the room becomes more inspired, and those working in that room are more likely to want to share the best of themselves without intimidation and fear.

In a recent discussion about this rule and the philosophy around embracing ideas and trying the "yes, and" out for size, I was asked, "Isn't there a place for just saying no?" I asked for an example, and one was shared. Challenge accepted.

Here was the example, "What if your team asks for $50,000 to celebrate a team's milestone? Do you have to be open to that if you don't have the budget?"

Here is how I approach that challenge and answered the question.

First thing I would do is consider to which part of that idea I can have an open mind. I look for the "yes" to then expand upon.

I look for possible parts of the idea where I can show alignment and openness to finding some solutions:

- Can I be open to celebrating a team's milestone?

- Can I be open to supporting the team member for wanting to recognize the team and celebrate?

Yes. I would suggest the answers to those questions are… yes.

Rather than being overly reactive to the budget request and jumping to the "no," I aim to challenge myself to build upon the underlying interest and seek ways to find some level of affirmation.

Is it a great idea that you want to celebrate a team's milestone?
- Yes, and I am totally supportive.

Are there other ways we can explore options together given our budget situation?
- Yes, and let's be creative around ways to fund what the team wants to do if they specifically want a big party.

Could we find a venue with no venue rental fee, like someone's backyard?
- Yes, and that would help us celebrate in a financially responsible way.

This technique challenges you and the team to look for ways to build off each other's ideas instead of easily land in the "no" to the initial request.

Look for yes. Look for ways to build upon ideas.

"Yes, and" towards ideas doesn't mean that every idea should be implemented. It doesn't mean that we must do everything and anything that is ever suggested. It means that we can explore a bit, we can help build people up instead of take people down. Positivity brings about positivity. Keep spirits up, keep confidences up, and that will keep those ideas flowing.

Activities: Get to work

For one of my favorite rules comes one of my favorite activities. The "Yes, and that means" activity.

Activity 4A. Yes, and that means, in pairs.

Instructions:
1. Start by again breaking into pairs.
2. Identify the person (Person A) who will start the exercise.
3. Agree on a question about something you did once that you will tackle together during this exercise; the following are a few examples:
   a. What did you do this past weekend?
   b. What did you do over the summer?
   c. What did you do yesterday?
4. Person A shares a first sentence (e.g., something done over the summer or over the past weekend, "I worked out").
5. Person B then starts their sentence with, "Yes, and that means," followed by a statement that might follow logically.
6. Person A and B then go back and forth for about two to three minutes.

Here's an example of what an exchange could sound like:

Person A: "I worked out over the weekend."
Person B: "Yes, and that means I'm pretty muscular right now."
Person A: "Yes, and that means I'm probably going to have to buy all new clothes."
Person B: "Yes, and that means I may need a second job to pay for those clothes."
Person A: "Yes, and that means I might have to work all the time."
Person B: "Yes, and that means I probably won't be able to work out anymore."
Person A: "Yes, and that means I'll probably lose all my muscle."

Person B: "Yes, and that means I probably won't need those new clothes."

Person A: "Yes, and that means I can sell those new clothes."

Person B: "Yes, and that means I'll have money to buy those new clothes."

Okay, you can take it in a lot of directions.

Time permitting, change partners and play again.

> *You can certainly start each sentence with the good old fashioned "yes, and." I have found that the "and that means" gives folks some more direction on what the next sentence could be, but feel free to decide and implement what you think will work with your group.*

Activity 4B. Yes, and that means, in broader group.

Instructions:

1. Once the group has run the activity in pairs and is more comfortable, four to six people can be called upon to come to the front of the room and run the exercise down the line, meaning right to left or left to right: Person A, Person B, Person C, and so on.

2. Person A shares the first sentence, answering one of those aforementioned questions.

3. Person B then shares the second sentence, beginning with, "Yes, and that means" before contributing to the answer to the question a bit more.

4. And so on and so forth through Person C, D, and E, then back to Person A; running the exercise for two to four minutes, depending on how the group is doing.

5. Take a few minutes to debrief as a broader team with questions such as:

   a. How did you feel knowing that you were not going to judge or negate the sentence before you? You only had one job in this exercise: start with "yes, and that means" and run with it, go with the flow.

b. Did you feel more positivity than usual in the space?

c. Were the creative juices flowing more steadily, knowing that you were on the same path with the other people, telling a bit of a story with an easy prompt to get the ideas going?

d. Imagine running this exercise and instead of "yes, and that means," you had to start your sentence with "no, that's not right." Try that approach as well for a few minutes and notice the difference in how the team feels, contradicting what is said beforehand.

Why do this:

- Opening the mind to the possibilities, leading with "yes, and" versus a "no" or a "yes, but" encourages teams to bring the best of themselves.
- Even a dose of small agreement can go a long way towards achieving an environment where people feel appreciated for their contribution.

Considerations

Consider the following benefit of this rule being applied in the workplace. This rule gives a team, or temporarily formed group of work professionals, a shared vocabulary.

One morning, I led an *Improv at Work* workshop for a team who would then also meet in the afternoon for their annual business planning working session.

During the business planning working session, one of the teammates shared a thought, another teammate furrowed her brow, and looked like she was about to shoot down the idea, but instead she said, "OK, how can I think about this in terms of 'yes, and'?"

She then offered up a question to understand the thought further, which put the room on a more collaborative path of welcoming ideas rather than being overly critical too soon.

Warnings

Despite all the caveats, some may continue to walk away from the "Yes, and that means" exercise or the "Yes, and" rule in general and think that the guidance here is to agree with everything said (back to a previous point made). In fact, and in practice, the activity and rule are more about creating an environment that embraces "the new" for exploration rather than about agreeing with everything and anything. This is an important distinction, especially for those who are more predisposed to the Lid way of thinking.

Every idea should not turn into action necessarily nor receive investment since some ideas are just that — ideas that may turn into options, which then a business may decide to favor or not favor, move forward or not move forward.

The essence of this rule is to — once again — welcome ideas versus shut them down prematurely. Welcome people to contribute ideas versus prevent that contribution. Motivate others versus stifle others.

Strike to find that right balance between open minds, creative work environments, intelligent business actions and decisions, and healthy skepticism. Recognize without open minds in a conference or board room, companies run the risk of only discussing a certain set of ideas, which may be too limited, too narrow, or too constrained for next-level innovation.

Reflections

At the end of each chapter with activities, take a few minutes, after you have practiced, and write down your thoughts.

You can either capture free-flowing thoughts on a separate piece of paper, digital notepad, or the lined text box provided here.

IX

THE GET OUT OF THE BACK OF YOUR HEAD RULE

Overview: What's the rule?

It is very easy to fall out of the moment in nearly every setting. I speak from firsthand experience.

It could be that you're talking to a friend, talking with a colleague, or talking to your boss. Your mind starts off listening, engaged in the dialogue, and then drifts to other thoughts, such as:

- Other work thoughts:
  - What do you need to do later for a work deliverable?
  - Should the team get on a call tonight to discuss?
- Traffic/commuting thoughts:
  - How much is traffic building outside; should you have taken the train today versus driven into work?
  - Should you have gone into work today instead of worked from home?

115

- Completely work-unrelated thoughts:
  - If you don't work out tonight, will you have time tomorrow?
  - If you were the kid in *Home Alone*, would you have gone to the store to buy a toothbrush?

It happens to all of us. Work-related topics or not, when your mind drifts during a work conversation, you are no longer in top form to carry on the conversation.

One common mind drift during a work discussion is real-time judgment on how you're doing in that discussion. Have you ever had any of the following thoughts while a conversation is still taking place with someone?

- Have I said enough?
- Have I said too much?
- Did I just say the right thing? The wrong thing?
- Did that sound smart?
- Are we spending too much time on this topic; should I move to the next topic prepared?

That critical judgment thinking, though rooted in wanting the discussion to be the best possible one, takes you away from the discussion itself. That thinking makes it difficult for you to be as constructive, thoughtful, and engaging as you could and would have been in the conversation. It may be that you can cover up those thoughts, so no one knows about the mental gymnastics happening behind your frontal cortex, but it may look like you're distracted, anxious, panicked, and ultimately, less credible. Those aren't great looks on anyone.

So, this particular rule is rooted in keeping you in the moment in a meaningful way. Keeping you present. Preventing non-constructive thought wandering. Preventing you from mentally retreating to the back of your mind with your thoughts and instead keeping your thoughts and attention in that space between you and another person. Visualize your attention and energy in that space. This will keep you in the moment where it matters in the human exchange of ideas!

You wouldn't physically walk out during an important meeting with a colleague so don't mentally do it.

In improv: How does it work in improv comedy?

When you're up on stage and the scene starts, you are *on*. There are no do-overs while all eyes from the audience are watching.

So, what happens if you are having a bad day? What if there is a lot going on in your personal life? What if someone is sick in your family? Your mind can't go to those places, not when you're on — your mind must be on stage, with your fellow actor — ready to go. Ready to act. Ready to *react*. Ready to serve up another line.

I alluded to this earlier, but to reiterate, think of it as though your focus and thoughts must be in the space between you and that other person, the other actor. All other worries must be left behind.

You're reading each other and are completely there for one another, in the moment. You're figuring out your relationship — what it has been and what is happening to that relationship in the scene that you are both creating that moment. You're identifying a conflict; you're deciding how you will resolve it together. The events are unfolding organically and comically, only when and if your focus and thoughts can live in that space between each other, together.

When you break from that, when your thoughts creep back to the very back of your mind, it can be very painful.

In improv, actors rehearse, but not to rehearse *lines* as that wouldn't be improvisational theatre. Instead, improv actors rehearse *experiences* to build the mental muscle which keeps the actors in that space together and prevents the actors from allowing their thoughts to migrate to the back of their heads, away from the moment, away from each other.

When a migration happens on stage, an actor then begins to worry: *What am I doing up here, what are we doing up here? What will our issue be and how are we going to resolve it? Will this be funny? Is it funny? Will the audience laugh and are they laughing yet? What should I say next? How long will this scene run?*

All this worry and doubt can lead to uncomfortable minutes on stage for the actor and all the actors involved in the scene. In fact, that angst can often be observed by the audience. It isn't difficult for the audience to recognize when an actor's thoughts have retreated away from the scene.

It is a much smoother experience on stage when both actors have leaned into the scene, leaned into the energy being shared on stage, and leaned away from those thoughts that could get them stuck.

At work: Why do we need it in the workplace?

I'm going to paint a picture of a work scenario, a rather common work scenario. In this scenario, you are about to meet with a colleague for the first time.

It could be your new boss, another leader in your organization, or it could be a new team member with whom you will start to work more closely on a project. Maybe you are meeting with a new customer or client. Imagine one of these meetings that represents an example most relevant to you and your line of work.

In advance, you did your homework. You researched the environment, you researched what could be top of mind for this person in their role, and you researched the roles this person may have held previously. You were prepared.

You put together some graphs or bullet points on topics that you believed were of interest to this person based on the research that you conducted and based on the industry in which you work.

You kicked off the meeting with an agenda, which you shared with the individual after polite pleasantries. You could tell that this person didn't have that much time, so you dove right into the materials and thoughts you prepared. Aligned to the topics, which you believed would be of interest to this person, you brought a few questions with you (shout out to the curiosity rule), and you had your own perspectives on those questions just in case.

It was clear that this person was kind, there were smiles, and it seemed as though this person was in a good mood.

However, it was also clear that this person was not interested in the three topics you prepared.

This lack of interest could be due to a number of reasons. This person was already well on their way down a journey with those topics and didn't need to talk about them further. This person had already conducted their own research. This person's role had changed further and did not require focus on those topics anymore.

Though this person was still a relevant person in your work sphere, you did not have the topics of interest to this person in your well-prepared graphs and bullet points.

Oh no, you thought, and probably other words flew through your cranial space.

The panic set in quickly. All of a sudden there was a whole new line of thought that pulled your focus into the dreaded back of your head, which we try to avoid when in collaborative discussions with others. You could experience the following thoughts back there:

- What do we talk about now?
- What will they want to know?
- I don't have any other materials with me.
- I don't have anything else to talk about.
- Will they want to talk to me about other things?
- What if they never want to talk to me again?
- What are they thinking about me right now?
- I have 55 more minutes in this 60-meeting appointment.
- Will there be another meeting?

Take several deep breaths. You may take one now if even the thought of this story brings back memories you have tried to suppress.

Instead of letting panic take hold of us in those moments, what if we took back the power. What if we took control and converted that stressed energy snowballing in the back of our heads to more positive, collaborative energy that could be sent back into the space between us and that other person? This is the perfect opportunity to focus on the room and the energy coming from the other person.

It feels much better to be a part of positive energy rather than wasting time exuding energy that is incredibly stressed.

Back to this example that was set up for you, how can you overcome the back of the head stress and panic?

First, if you prepared, you might have a few other topics that will come to mind, but maybe not. In that case, it is fine to reset the workplace stage with this person. You could recognize that you brought a few areas or hypotheses, but that there may be other things to talk about together, maybe other areas of excitement or concern for this person in a new role? It is okay to capture those topics during the meeting along with a follow-up to do some refreshed research and thinking, then come back together within a reasonable period of time.

Unfortunately, more times than not, this catapult into the unknown, (improvised) world causes much stumble and discomfort for most work professionals and so we turn to the improv world to learn how improv actors get more comfortable in that space away from the back of the head and toward a healthier, creative space that can lead to new ideas, collaborative energy, and most importantly, comfort for all.

Activity: Get to work

Given the mental athletics required to keep you in the moment with other people and prevent you from the mental retreat to the back of your head, let's serve up two activities for your teams to practice. Find one that you like with your team and practice, practice, practice. It's like working out a muscle at the gym, you must work on this one, over and over again.

Activity 5A. Headlines, "This Just In."

It's time to practice with a game that forces you to be in the moment with another person. This activity is one where you must listen to what the other person says instead of trying to craft your sentence while they're talking.

Before we get to the activity, I want you to think about a specific time in most meetings when we do not all do a great job of listening because we're too busy thinking about our next comment. That time is during introductions with an ice breaker.

These are the introduction ice breakers when we're asked to say our name, perhaps our role on a team, and then answer some question about ourselves.

The first person starts and then we go around the room asking each person to answer that same question.

Why might we be set up to fail during these introduction exercises?

Typically, here is what happens. First, the ice breaker is explained: each person will be asked a question, going around the physical or virtual room. What happens next is that each person then stresses about what they are going to say, so they only partially listen to the others' answers until finally they have had their turn — and they can relax.

We still use these introduction ice breakers, but it is helpful to acknowledge that one objective of an ice breaker is to, yes, give you a chance to introduce yourself and wow everyone with your answer to, "what's your favorite thing to do on a Saturday" or "what is the word that describes you best," but another objective is for you to listen to others to get to know them better and form connections.

"You like to sleep in on Saturdays sometimes all the way to Sundays, me too."

"Or you like to study the rare mating habits of the domestic free-range squirrel at parks nearby, me too."

We really need to help people find better hobbies.

So, let's start by playing a game in which you must listen — you must visualize yourself actually in the space between you and the other person.

Instructions:
1. Stand in a circle or sit around a table in a group of about five people.
2. One person, Person A, is identified as the starting person.
3. Person A starts off by saying and pointing to the next person, Person B, "This just in…" and then gives a fictitious statement that is non-politically charged, nor offensive in any way. Person B can be anyone in the circle, not necessarily the person next to Person A.
4. Person B then points to someone else, Person C, and starts off their headline by saying, "This just in…" with an equally fictitious, non-politically charged statement, however their headline must be in some way connected to the headline shared by Person A; it cannot

just be something that Person B already had in mind and is in no way connected. For example:

   a. Person A may say, "This just in, aliens land on top of Mount Rushmore, completely confused as they introduce themselves to the presidential mountains and are met with silence."

   b. Person B, who must take some inspiration from Person A's headline, may say, "This just in, mountain climbers around the world cheer as gravity defying boots allow for much easier climbs."

5. Person C then continues, handing off to anyone else in the same manner. Person D or going around the circle, the next person also will give a headline, yet use a word or concept from the previous person.

6. For example: "This just in, baby saves polar bear in the wild with a spare pacifier and compliment." Then next person: "This just in, polar bear spotted in downtown Iowa City; citizens confused and blame global warming."

Why do this:

*   The rules of this activity force you to stay in the moment with the other people; you need their statement before you can put together your own.
*   You can't prepare; that might be scary for some, but others may find it liberating — enjoy the liberation.
*   It's fun to play this game which should remind you, in a calm, light-hearted way, to listen to one another and recognize that we need people in conversations to advance thinking fully.

Activity 5B. Can you count one to 21, altogether?

It sounds easy, but wait, there's more.

I'll start off by saying, I love this next activity. For one thing, it takes people out of their comfort zones, which I personally find entertaining.

Secondly, I will say, I'm always surprised by the fact that every team I have facilitated has figured out a way to reach the finish line, despite some believing it's impossible.

Instructions:
1. In groups of about five to seven, stand in a circle. It really does work best when folks are standing, but if that does not work easily, please sit around a table or sit in a circle without a table.
2. Establish the goal, to count from one to 21, which sounds fairly easy.
3. Here's the kicker: one person will start by saying out loud "One" — now, without any social cues, someone else from the circle will say "Two."
4. If more than one person says the next number together, you all start over, back to One.
5. Once you get through "Two" with only one voice, someone else will say "Three" and so on. Each time, if more than one person says the number with another person, the team starts over, back to One.

It might sound like: one, two, three (more than one person says three)... back to one, two, three, four (more than one person says four)... back to one, two... and so on until you manage to get to 21.

As I said, each team with whom I've worked has made it to 21! You must believe! I believe in you.

Why do this:
- The key to this game is to feel the energy of the team around you.
- You must imagine yourself sitting in the middle of the circle, sensing if someone is going to say something.
- I dare you to try to get yourself stuck in the back of your head.
- You can't easily!

Considerations

I have been a part of project workshops that have seemed scary to me because I had hit a part of the day where I started to panic that we would not figure out what to do next. Projects like, reducing a product development timeline or redefining the geographic footprint for a function.

When you start to get stuck in your head and doubts fill up, that is the time when you need to focus on the room and energy from the group. You are not alone, and there is power in that awareness.

There is power being a part of the positive energy you find from others rather than giving off a panicked energy. This activity will flex the muscle that keeps you in tune with that power and can keep you (mentally) in the room.

These activities are fun. They have goals and shared successes as you'll find in real life as well.

Warnings

This is an important warning… being in the moment and not in the back of your head, does not mean that you should abandon good thinking that you already did to prepare for the discussion. You might in fact need to "rack your brain" or recall what you had previously prepared, absolutely.

You can retrieve notes, you can take a reflective moment to remember what you read previously and thought about sharing in the discussion yet prioritized the topics that unfortunately are not serving you as well as you would have liked. You simply (not so simply) want to avoid retreating to panic and anxiety-ridden thinking that in fact slows down the progression of the conversation and is more likely to take that conversation to a grinding halt.

The point to emphasize is that you are not alone in a conversation, and it is possible that your best way through a bumpy part of a conversation may be to also recognize that you are not alone in figuring out how.

Know your stuff. Be in the moment and stay there.

Reflections

At the end of each chapter with activities, take a few minutes, after you have practiced, and write down your thoughts.

You can either capture free-flowing thoughts on a separate piece of paper, digital notepad, or the lined text box provided here.

X

THE WORK TO YOUR OBJECTIVES RULE

Overview: What's the rule?

Simply put, this rule asks you to know why you set out to do something, align with others, and keep that end in mind. Simple.

I would end this rule overview section right now except that it's never that simple. So, let's break down the rule in its three parts.

First, know why you're setting out to do something. When you are engaging with a person or group, make note of the purpose of the engagement. This can come in the form of a purpose statement, a list of meeting objectives, or desired meeting outcomes. It's more than an agenda; it's a way to articulate *what good looks like* coming out of your time together.

Second, align with others. It's okay if you have a set of objectives and another person has a different set, as long as you discuss that at the start and get aligned before the discussion begins. Using a house analogy between a couple, if one of you wants to talk about wallpaper for your first-floor bathroom, yet the other one wants to talk about neighborhoods in which to buy a house, you might not be on the same page for the discussion. Take the time to align in advance; take the time to agree on a common set of objectives even if one of the objectives is to resolve some differences.

Finally, keep the end in mind. Remember why you are in the discussion by reflecting on the meeting's purpose throughout the discussion. Remember what you are all seeking from the time together. Avoid distractions; avoid Lid behaviors. Acknowledge that it is common and exciting to be agile during discussions, allowing you and a team to change course in real-time. However, be intentional if you and the team shift your objectives. Be overt about it. It should be a thoughtful redirection in the conversation versus an unfocused move.

In improv: How does it work in improv comedy?

On the stage, the initial set of outcomes for a scene are high-level, but clear. Figure out how to be entertaining and interesting for a few minutes. There is more to it though.

Actors set a few goals for themselves when they're up on stage together beyond the obvious top two. Those goals include, but are not limited to the following:
1. Be funny.
2. Don't fall down unintentionally.
3. Support your fellow actors to be successful.
4. Create an interesting storyline.
5. Create the scene path and a resolution such that the scene arcs up to something and then comes to a natural conclusion. You don't want the audience scratching their head wondering, "Are they done?" They should know when it is over. Scene.
6. Don't burp in the middle of a word nor spit in another actor's face.
7. Don't offend anyone or otherwise in any way cross the line between being funny and being unnecessarily rude.
8. Don't break character (unless you really can't help it).

9. Finally, and while you are still fully present on stage and in your scene, remember to apply all these improv rules, *all the time.*

There's so much an actor is trying to do up there!

At work: Why do we need it in the workplace?

The workplace thrives on objectives, goals, guiding principles, and lessons learned. Objectives. In theory the workplace should exist, because it is an environment built by a goal or an objective. It improves since it is an environment that learns from the past. However, there are a few breakdowns in how people execute.

For one thing, in the workplace, objectives are not always clear to an individual nor a team. Let's analyze.

Cue up scary movie music.

You found yourself in a meeting… no you led a workshop. This workshop had people from different functional groups joining, some in person, some via videoconference.

You started the workshop with an ice breaker, a warm-up. I'm so proud you warmed up. The session was going well; people were becoming increasingly more comfortable in the discussions and with one another. Some were chuckling during the ice breaker as they eased themselves into talking with people with whom they didn't normally converse.

It was going well.

Or so you thought.

Then you started the next part of the workshop: brainstorming. Some were interested in it right away and dove into the brainstorm. Others were confused.

Then, it happened.

Someone stood up in the back.

You saw this person stand up.

This person looked at you and the rest of the group and uttered the words you fear most in these workshops. Dreadful words. Dreadful words were uttered that you have not heard uttered in a workshop in seven years. You knew it had been seven years, because it left a seven-year workshop scar.

You heard, "What are we doing here? What are we trying to get out of this session? I don't get it."

Nooooo. What did you do wrong?

Suddenly, faces around the room shifted from happy to perplexed, from relaxed to puzzled. There was a divide in the room that was not sensed previously. Some had been engaged and now questioned that engagement; some had been quietly confused all along and now a spokesperson for that confusion had emerged.

How did you get to this place?

Could you crawl under the table like you imagined yourself doing seven years ago?

Probably not.

You paused and reflected on the situation. Where did it go wrong? You assumed the group knew why you were in the room together and what you all set out to achieve.

You assumed this and therefore were unclear. You did not cover a set of clear objectives for the session. You did not get feedback on those objectives before asking the participants to jump into the heart of the workshop. It wasn't clear: what did you intend for folks to get out of the workshop, what was everyone being asked to contribute during the workshop, and what outcomes could they expect from it? How does this workshop fit into a broader set of activities or goals for this team, for the broader organization?

You skipped those parts and jumped into the discussions, but not everyone followed. Some likely understood the unspoken objectives, some were just nice. Some didn't follow and would speak up to say, "What are we doing here?"

To move together in harmony and with creativity it is critical to agree on a set of objectives with all those involved, so you are all marching down the same path.

It is important to set clear objectives, both individually and as a group, and it is equally important to set objectives that are sufficient and detailed enough to mean something, as well as to help the group understand what success looks like when you reach an endpoint such as the end of a meeting or the end of a phase of work.

What do I mean? Let's test some objective examples in a game show I like to call: "Name Your Objective — Enough or Not Enough." You may already hear the 1960's game show music playing in your head to set the stage.

How do we play?

I'll explain. It's simple. We'll give you a possible discussion objective and you call out, "Enough or Not Enough." If the objective is considered "Enough," the objective sufficiently represents a goal for a discussion that is clear and will help progress a topic, relationship, or expectation of a multiperson exchange of words and ideas. If the objective is considered "Not Enough," that objective does not have enough specificity, information, nor detail to guide the participants towards the progression, relationship-building, or expectation. Let's get started.

Name Your Objective: Enough or Not Enough.

Is this objective enough or not enough?

Round One: *"Get through the discussion to the end of the meeting."*

Commentary, your inner monologue:
Interesting. It does seem to be clear with respect to where you want the meeting to go. You want to reach the end of it. But do you think it sufficiently represents a true goal for a meeting and will it advance a topic or relationship? No. This objective is not enough.

Final answer: Not enough.

Judges Say:
You are correct. Though we can appreciate the (lack of) creativity that went into this objective, it clearly is insufficient for a team to activate towards a business goal or outcome. As long as the clock on the meeting time runs out, a team may reach the end of the meeting, but did they really advance anything? Was the purpose achieved? No, not so much. It's like declaring an objective for a grocery shopping trip is that the trip has a start and an end. We would all agree that is not enough of an objective since it is likely that the intent of that trip was to bring something home from the store. This type of an objective is not enough. Insufficient.

Is this objective enough or not enough?

Round Two: *"Align on a list of key stakeholders for your project and an action plan to meet with each one and understand each stakeholder's priorities."*

Commentary, your inner monologue:

This one seems different than the objective in Round One. Clear, specific, and action-oriented. Does it help when the participants understand what is expected of them to progress a topic?

Yes, it does.

Final answer: It's enough.

Judges Say:

You are correct again. Now we're talking. It is clear what this team is trying to do together, what the discussion should include, a clear set of next steps associated with the objective. Love it. Clear objective. And, there is enough detail in the objective to guide the group sufficiently toward what they need to do in the meeting in order to progress following the meeting.

We could play this game all day, or I could at least, mainly because it is an easy game. Amazing then, isn't it, that so many still have trouble setting clear, sufficient objectives.

With this newfound appreciation and awareness of objectives, I would ask that you first review your own calendar and ask yourself if the objectives are clearly and sufficiently defined for each discussion you have scheduled or plan to attend. Then ask yourself if those objectives have been or will be shared with others. If any of those questions require some objective work, set an objective to focus on objectives.

Activities: Get to work

In addition to the game above, which asked if objectives were clear, sufficient, and shared, let's explore an activity which practices the art of making sure you are actively working towards those objectives when it matters. This one can be practiced for the workplace, but it is also one that you can play with friends, school-aged children, older children, older adults, as well as nearly everyone.

The goal of this activity is to work in pairs and go back and forth advancing a dialogue, but where the first letter of the first word of the sentence will go through the alphabet as you go back and forth as a pair. That is the objective. Follow the objective, follow the alphabet.

You must navigate a discussion where the starring role is in fact our very own alphabet. Read on for more details.

Activity 6. The ABCs of a conversation.

Instructions:
1. Pick a partner; your team can also work in slightly larger groups if the numbers allow.
2. Agree on a location or relationship to get the scene going.
3. Person A starts, and the first letter of the first word in the sentence starts with the letter A or the pair can pick any letter of the alphabet and start there.
   a. For instance: "Annie just walked out of class with my coat."
4. Person B must then advance the discussion, with the only rule that the first letter of the first word in their sentence must start with B (or the next letter in the alphabet no matter where they started).
   a. Building upon the example below, Person B might say, "But I thought you gave her that coat earlier today."
5. Try to tell a story in this dialogue or at least try to have a dialogue that makes sense. The sentences together should flow instead of not flow, in which case the sentences come across completely disconnected, an exchange of random thoughts. Your objective is to continue through the alphabet in a conversation that is coherent, and you get bonus points if it's interesting. Note, there are no bonus points for you competitive folks out there. But please hear "job well done" in your head for those who need it.
   a. Further to the example, Person A might now say, "Coats don't grow on trees; I said she could borrow a pencil which by the way sounds nothing like, 'Take my coat, please.'"

The following is a more fluid example of what this exchange might sound like through more letters of the alphabet; the relationship applied here is that between a dog and the dog owner. That is right, you can pick any relationship, so have fun with it.

Person A: "Albert, I've noticed that, though I always seem to be served the same pebble-shaped food in a bowl each day, every day, your meals vary by color and texture. I'd like to file a complaint."

Person B: "But we've been together for six years, and you've never said anything."

Person A: "Come on, I've given plenty of looks."

Person B: "Dreadfully sorry, good friend; let's brainstorm what I can do differently."

Person A: "Eat my food for a week, and I'll eat yours."

Person B: "For a week?"

And so on and so forth.

Have fun with it. If you spin through the alphabet rather quickly, you can always go through it one more time.

Considerations

This activity takes a strict stand on setting an objective. The objective in this activity is: follow the flow of the alphabet.

Consider the intent of this activity, there is power in setting objectives for what you are doing and what you are asking others to do. It is both reassuring and calming to know what good looks like. In this activity it's clear. In real life, we try to make it clear.

How do we try? Sometimes someone sends out meeting objectives in advance, so they are written down for clarity and traceability. Other times objectives are presented at the start of the meeting. In practice those objectives are not revisited enough during a meeting to ensure the group is still on the path toward achieving those objectives. In practice those objectives are not consistently reviewed at the end of the meeting to see if a next step should be captured if the full set of objectives haven't been achieved by the meeting's wrap-up (which by the way should not be seen as a failure… perhaps the group simply needs more time to process, discuss, and reach that objective).

In the alphabet game, each player must think about the objective before they speak; the objective is in the forefront of their brain each time they come up with a sentence to relay back to the other player. In real life, the objective may not be in the forefront each time someone contributes to the dialogue, which is fine and appropriate. So, support your team, support the participants, support the objectives, and revisit what you all set out to do: before a break, before you move on to another part of the meeting and/or at the end of the meeting for confirmation and any course correction required.

Warnings

Two warnings.

First, it is important to remember your objectives and align with others, respecting they may have objectives as well. Just as you have a desired outcome, they too may have desired outcomes and collaborating on objectives is a positive first step on the road to broader collaborations. In most cases, even during times when you are expected to "own the meeting," I'd ask if it could be appropriate for you to share the objectives and agenda in advance for feedback. You will then start your discussion journey truly aligned.

Second, it is possible that you and others both need to adjust those objectives during the discussion if the discussion requires some agility based on what you are all working through, talking about, or exploring together. That is okay, too. You do not need to be too rigid with objectives as though you are all on a train with no ability to slow down or change the course of the tracks. If you do need to alter the objectives of the meeting to allow for greater flexibility, please do so together with the group, acknowledging that is what is happening and take the time to realign on that new set of objectives. The key is to understand the inputs, new information, or feedback requiring a change and seeing that change as a positive step towards advancing.

Reflections

At the end of each chapter with activities, take a few minutes, after you have practiced, and write down your thoughts.

You can either capture free-flowing thoughts on a separate piece of paper, digital notepad, or the lined text box provided here.

XI

THE TRUST YOUR TEAM RULE

Overview: What's the rule?

If you trust your team, show up like you do. Act like you do.

This rule does assume that trust is there. If trust is *not* there, I'd recommend an additional separate series of actions for a team or pair of individuals starting by asking questions to understand why it's absent and then what can be done to build it up.

It is most helpful in our interactions to ensure that we are living and breathing the trust that we have in each other and not just talking about that trust.

I have seen environments where the phrase "I trust you" is used, though the actions that follow seem to suggest otherwise.

"I trust you, but I'll still micro-manage to make sure it gets done well."

"I trust you, but I'll still run a parallel process on the side in case you really mess things up."

And so on. We'll explore more of this contradiction a bit later.

If you do trust your team, trust your team. It's not enough to say the words. If you trust the team, your actions should be the demonstration and representation of the trust. When people hear, see, and feel the trust, they are more likely to feel comfortable bringing out the best of themselves. That's what we want. Trust the process!

In improv: How does it work in improv comedy?

Before going on stage for an improv show or for a scripted play, a cast stands together, typically standing around in a circle, but most shapes work. After completing the warm-ups we talked about previously, and either with words or with their eyes, the cast communicates, "I got you." You don't feel alone going into a show. I've never felt alone going into a show with other actors. Together, you will not let one another down.

An actor feels the support of the other actors on stage. The actors are a machine together, all rise up or all crash down (figuratively). Actors have each other's backs. They are casts. They are teams. They are families. They enter the stage unified, together with one key ingredient built during countless rehearsal hours; that ingredient without which it all falls apart. The key ingredient included that brings them all together with a sense of security and comfort. *Trust.*

At work: Why do we need it in the workplace?

Instead of starting with what trust looks like, feels like, or how it is established, let's look at what the lack of trust looks like in the workplace since this lack of trust shows up in different ways, almost like personas. Think about your own teams and relationships; think about whether or not you see these personas in you or those around you in your work life.

Persona One: Trusting in denial.

What it sounds like:

"Of course, I trust you. Except if you must answer a question on behalf of our team, in which case I'll let you go ahead and answer since you already started to talk. Then I'll kind of interrupt you and answer the question anyway, in my words, though arguably my answer will sound quite similar to what you said. However, I'll think my answer is needed and better than yours. I'll also believe that the person who asked the question is surely to understand now that I've stomped all over what you said and had to add my bit. But, of course, I trust you completely."

Persona Two: Trusting with back-up plans.

"Of course, I trust you. Except if I really need something to get done that you are qualified to do. However, I'm not sure, so I'll ask a few other people to work on the same thing in parallel just in case you completely mess it up. I'm sure you won't mess up since I trust you, but I will have options to protect myself, our team, and the universe from your epic failures. But, of course, I trust you completely."

Persona Three: Trusting myself only.

"Of course, I trust you. Except, even though you are qualified and have more time than I do to complete this task, plus it's more in your job description than mine, I'm going to take this one myself, so it's completed up to my standards. I'll also take this other thing, because I'm really the only person who could possibly understand the request and therefore really the only person best positioned to do the work. Well, at least to do the work correctly. But, of course, I trust you completely, in case you were wondering."

Persona Four: I don't trust you. (Version of Persona Three, just more direct.)

"Of course, I really don't trust you nor do I trust anyone. It's not you, it's me. I have trust issues. You see, I've let people work on things for me before, and I always seem to be disappointed, so I've learned that it's best not to trust anyone and try to build meaningful professional relationships other ways. So, though I do not trust you, I hope we can build the best possible work relationship with the comfort and confidence needed to bring creativity and innovation to our business." (At least this person was the most honest about where their trust truly resides — nowhere.)

So, at the heart of this rule is the fact that trust is the necessary ingredient in building meaningful relationships, despite what Persona Four may wish to believe.

There is real work that goes into trust, so it would trick no one to suggest that an improv rule is enough to build trust. In order to build trust with your colleagues and teams, first of all, you need to know your stuff and bring it. You also need to show up for other people consistently, check your ego at the door, be vulnerable in some cases, be honest with others about your strengths and areas of development, acknowledge, and at times, prioritize others' needs and interests above your own. There are books, talks, experts, and working sessions: you can get help in the trust department if you reach out.

Working with a team, it's okay to talk about trust; it doesn't need to be this intangible "secret sauce" that either exists or doesn't. It's okay to acknowledge there's history for that team such that the team needs to work on trusting one another. A team may choose to have a heart-to-heart and brainstorm a path to bring trust back. People say trust takes a lot of time to build, but not much time to break down. That may be true, yet ignoring a trust issue and hoping it just resolves itself, makes for a more stressful work environment in the short term and a shakier path to building that trust back again. Lean in to trust; it is the secret sauce in the workplace, and that secret sauce should be in the spotlight, not behind the curtain.

Activity: Get to work

A team focusing on trust may wish to bring an improv activity into a regularly scheduled touchpoint, queue activity!

This activity pushes the boundaries of trust for a team. It puts the statement out there: do we really trust each other to shape the path ahead of us? Fortunately for all, the shape ahead is in the form of some fun scene work, so no real risks are on the table except the risk of having fun, and perhaps, making fun of one another, which always comes with the risk of embarrassment if we let it, and *only* if we let it. So, don't let it, no need to be embarrassed, we're all friends here. And even if we're not all friends… well, make sure no one is taping any of it. Recording devices should be nowhere in sight.

Activity 7. Screenwriter.

Instructions:
1. Divide into groups of four to five people.
2. Assign a character to one of the members of the group as the "Screenwriter."
3. The screenwriter should sit to the side and hold in front of them an imaginary typewriter. If you're unfamiliar with one of those, fine, imagine it's a laptop. Either prop will work in the imaginary world. Grab your imaginary quill, ink, and scroll.
4. The rest of the characters line up facing the room.
5. A location or relationship is picked for the group.
6. The screenwriter begins to tell the story, with "Once upon a time," miming typing on the typewriter or laptop (or acting out writing on a scroll) when they speak.
7. The screenwriter may choose to introduce one character at a time or begin with some or all as the imagination spirit moves them; for example, here are a few possible openers:
    a. "Once upon a time, it was a dark and humid night, a set of grandparents were standing in line waiting for the box

office to open so that they could purchase *Disney on Ice* tickets for their 10 grandkids, when someone over a loudspeaker announced you could only purchase two kid tickets per family." One asked, "How can we possibly decide who we should take?" The other then said...

8. The actors in front of the room then pick up wherever the screenwriter takes a pause, picking up from the opener above, one of the actors may say:

   a. "To make this decision, we should imagine telling each one that we have a ticket for them and consider what they might say to that news."

      i. A third actor then comes up pretending to be the first grandchild, perhaps selfish, perhaps kind — and so on and so forth through as many grandkids as they'd like to go through.

9. The screenwriter may take hold of the scene whenever they like, interrupting ever so gently until the back and forth (screenwriter to actors to screenwriter to actors) allows a scene to emerge and then come to a conclusion. The facilitator calls "scene" where so inclined.

Why do this:

- It reminds us that at work, for most of us, we are not alone.

- Instead of that being a nervous fact, it can be exciting when there is trust with those around you and the knowledge that if a problem seems unsolvable, it probably means you need some help, and it's time to call upon your trusted work friends to join your crusade towards a set of options or answers.

- Unleashing the power of trust may take you and your colleagues into situations that you could not have imagined alone nor addressed alone. In fact, maybe that trust will take you to successes you might never have imagined.

Considerations

Consider easy ways to get the scene started with some canned storyline openers. In previous workshops, I have brought this activity into different kinds of team dynamics (new versus more established) with individuals with varying levels of comfort (calm versus terrified). Consider a fun way to jump-start this activity by asking your storyteller to start by describing a fairy tale or well-known tale — just to get started. Then the storyteller and the participants may branch away from that storyline to take a different, new journey.

The side effect of working through this activity is team bonding. In addition to putting trust in action by creating a story together, leaning on one another to develop a purpose, characters, resolution, and the experience of doing this activity as a mini team is bonding in and of itself. No matter what happens: great scene, a bomb of a scene (not in a good way), no matter what happens, you all did something you probably haven't done together and created something unique. Making this exercise a great one for new teams, existing teams refreshing the fun, existing teams with a few new members — a great exercise for just about any team. Have fun with it.

Warnings

Ok. Now the trust around trust. I would be remiss if I didn't suggest the following. It's true, you can't throw trust around like it's a just another word. It's earned and can be built, lost, and destroyed, or at least damaged as mentioned previously. As much as you need to build trust with others by bringing out the best version of you, showing up consistently, and putting the needs of others beside or ahead of your own, you should be aware whether other people are doing the same for you.

No sense in trusting someone who isn't qualified to perform a task, no sense in trusting someone who isn't there for you most of the time and isn't concerned with areas of greatest concern to you.

So, work on trust, aim to build trust and be the best you can be when you do trust someone: show them, live it, and invest in growing that trust. Eyes wide open though. Trust is a form of currency at the end of the day — it can be depreciated, so be aware — it can also be earned and grown with benefits that reap dividends.

Reflections

At the end of each chapter with activities, take a few minutes, after you have practiced, and write down your thoughts.

You can either capture free-flowing thoughts on a separate piece of paper, digital notepad, or the lined text box provided here.

XII

LIGHTS, CAMERA, TAKE ACTION

Let the preparations for improv at work begin.

Let's be serious, you wouldn't believe me if I said that the best way to succeed in a critical team brainstorm or a session with the CEO is only to play zip-zap-zop and get a good night's sleep.

The improv mindset and the rules are part of a multi-step plan towards achieving increased innovation and improved business outcomes.

Step One: Know the content.
The preparation for any collaborative session or presentation takes meaningful aggregation of the content itself. It may mean you need time to put structure around the conversation or it may mean that you need time to interview stakeholders, collect data, review iterations of your presentation plan, create the storyline, and review that with others — the list goes on and on. You'll bring the improv rules into the preparation process, yes, but improv rules cannot make up for poor preparation of the content.

Step Two: Bring the comfort and confidence.
Just as preparation includes the assembly of the right content, messaging, and details, you must ensure the right amount of preparation is going into

your own personal level of comfort and confidence to deliver that content and messaging in a meaningful way.

Just as comfort and confidence are required for standing up in front of an audience and doing improvisational comedy, those are required when you're in front of or standing alongside any "audience." So, get prepared. Your preparation may include standing in front of a mirror to practice what you want to say in the session, or it may include practicing with your team using activities associated with the improv rules in a quarterly team meeting. Take the time to build up your individual and collective levels of comfort and confidence.

Step Three: Repeat.
One cannot undervalue the benefits of strong preparation in Steps One and Two. Follow this approach each time, every time. Once a session or meeting begins, you know what you know (content), and you will feel the way you feel (comfort and confidence). So, walk into that environment with the best possible foot forward. We do our best in meetings to course correct, yes, but it is often difficult to course correct yourself out of poor preparation.

Let's talk about course correction. I recently found myself joining a work friend's contentious brainstorming meeting as a bystander; the meeting included participant defensiveness and offensiveness. I was later asked by my work friend, the meeting facilitator, for some feedback regarding their facilitation. What could they have done differently?

First, I shared the following story.

When my son was about four, he had a temper tantrum in a restaurant. There were arms flailing around; he was screaming and crying. A fork may have hit the floor with bits of macaroni and cheese going airborne. It's a blur.

My husband and I were helpless. We tried to do as much damage control as possible in the moment, but we barely survived the whole dinner. Fortunately, fellow restaurant patrons weren't given judging cards to raise as we left. I can imagine in our version of "Dining with the Cohens," surely, we would have been voted out of the restaurant.

I have thought about that experience over time and related it to a rough meeting. What could we have done differently in the restaurant to turn the situation around? Not much.

We're quick to give feedback on an experience itself, but often survival is the best-case scenario. How could the restaurant situation have been better? Better preparation. There wasn't much we could do during the situation, but there were actions we could have taken beforehand to have set us up for a more successful meal.

We should have been clear in the car about what good behavior looks like and that only *good* behavior is expected from all of us. We could have been more specific with our son about what happens if there is bad behavior, and at what point we will just walk out of the restaurant before being asked to leave, even without macaroni and cheese ingested.

> *Parents reading this are hopefully laughing at this since we all know there is no recipe for guaranteed good behavior — though it lives in our imaginations.*

Back to my work example, after sharing this story to the meeting facilitator, I asked what kind of pre-meeting preparation might have helped the meeting itself.

Content:
- Were materials co-developed with any of the meeting participants?
- Was the final set of materials shared in advance to get participants thinking about their questions versus being surprised during the meeting?
- Was the agenda shared in advance with time to incorporate feedback?

- Was all data collected in advance, also avoiding surprises?

Comfort and confidence:
- Did each team member warm up individually, mentally, and physically?
- Did the team leading the session warm up together?
- Was it clear to all meeting participants what would happen after the meeting, so folks knew what they needed to do in this meeting to make sure those next steps could be taken?

When this preparation is done thoughtfully, the environment is better set up to collaborate, communicate, and innovate versus worry about where they are in our discussions, what they want to get out of it, and where they are going next. Just the kind of worries that we try to avoid on the improv stage as well!

Improv rules and optimizing human-to-human interaction is a complement to the work that goes into being a subject matter expert, knowing your content. It doesn't cover up gaps and surely alone it isn't enough to make for meaningful engagement.

What these rules aim to do is to make your ability to interact and communicate more comfortable, more energetic, and more likely to result in true innovative outcomes, in whatever ways that means something to you, your business, as well as your business' customers, consumers, and businesses.

Getting Started, Getting Going: Call to Action

Now is the time to start the journey for yourself and for your team towards a better workplace. We agreed we spend plenty of time working and can be in control of how that time is spent.

To help you get started, consider the following five-step call to action.

1. Write down what you want to get out of improv that will help your team currently with their immediate needs. Ask yourself questions such as:

   - Are you and your team meeting new business collaborators so it would be helpful to increase levels of comfort in engaging new people, starting up conversations and building new relationships?
   - Do you need to improve the current team dynamic to promote team member inclusivity and creativity?
   - In general, is there a need to create a more positive work environment to engage new and existing team members in order to bring the best out of themselves?
   - Are you bringing a team together in-person for the first time or for the first time in a while and want to dust off those in-person human interaction skills?

2. Identify the first rule you could bring into your team's discussion.

   - For example, if you're coming together as a team for the first time in-person, you might want to pick the "warm-up" rule or the "get out of the back of your head" rule to enjoy being with each other fully, comfortably and completely present.
   - Whatever rule you pick, be deliberate around why it was chosen and share that reasoning with the others.

3. Pick an activity to practice with the team.

   - Explain the activity so that everyone understands the instructions and is comfortable proceeding.
   - Remind the team the point of the activity is simply to reinforce the rule. Shake out the nerves and any apprehension.

4. Debrief thoroughly as a team, including which new vocabulary terms you might bring more often into the team discussions.
   - New terms or phrases for the team may include, "avoid Lid behavior" and "yes, and."
   - Share the rule, activity and especially the new vocabulary with those outside the meeting. Pass it on.

5. Repeat steps one through four with the next important area on which to focus as a team.

Take the time to work on these elements; build the rules and the activities into your team calendar. Human interaction skills are no longer "nice to haves" — these are *the* skills that separate the extraordinary from the ordinary. The humans from the robots.

So, become extraordinary. Be human. Inspire yourself. Inspire others. Get out there — go for it. Stretch yourself.

Put improv to work. Bring improv to work. Expect greatness.

ACKNOWLEDGMENTS

How could I not thank the humans with whom I interacted during the development of this book on the topic of human interactions.

First, I am grateful for my husband, Mike, who reminds me all the time that I can do anything. With his love and support over the years (since our days at Northwestern University), I'm starting to believe that's true. He has listened to my beliefs on this topic and my reinforcing stories for years. He helped me refine language in the book to ensure a "non-theatre" person would still get it and let me know if I went too on-and-on about a certain idea (he likes to tell me that in person too).

He challenges me every day to believe in *myself* as much as *he* believes in me.

Next, to my children Zach and Sabrina. You've been there each step of the way as I've written this book. I've appreciated your perspectives on improv and your willingness to play so many of the games shared in this book. I can only imagine how you'll bring these lessons into whatever you do. You keep me on my toes in our discussions, forcing me to keep my own improv skills sharp, and you bring an abundance of joy and laughter into our house beyond what I could have believed possible.

To my mom and sister, growing up in a very theatre family shaped the person I am. I was raised to speak up and to be brave with my words, as well as my interactions. I was raised to believe in the impossible because anything is possible on stage, so why not in real life? You have both listened to me over the years as I've shaped my thoughts on this topic, you have sent me articles and books to read, and reviewed my own words. Thank you for being there for me each step of the journey towards this book.

If there was ever someone who would have gotten the biggest kick out of this book, it would be my dad. I used to talk to him about the concepts and listen to his thoughts on what has happened to human interaction skills over his lifetime. We would compare stories about our experiences watching how the general public has shifted to communicating via devices and away from live conversations and the impact it would have on our society. He never shifted away from live conversations, not my dad.

My dad taught me by showing me how to talk to people and how to treat people. He brought humor, humility, and kindness to everyone he met. He was one of the best humans I have ever known. I would say he would be so proud of me for sharing the thoughts in this book with the world — but then he told me he was proud of me every day just for being me.

Thank you to Arjun Bedi and Carol Lee Mitchell for believing in me enough to let me run my first two *Improv at Work* workshops with your teams. And thank you to Heather McIntire who reviewed chapters word-for-word with thoughtful feedback I would only expect from an analytical and critical thinker of her caliber.

Thank you to Donna Peters for the broad career and theatre/work discussions over the years and for the connection to Melanie Johnson and Jenn Foster from Elite, I'm eternally grateful. Big thank you, of course, to Melanie and Jenn as well.

And to Eileen Conery, editor extraordinaire. Not only did she help me by editing the book as only she can, she also spent time really pontificating on this topic, sharing her own experiences with me, and reinforcing why this book is so relevant to the entire workplace, across industries and functions, as well as why absolutely now is the time.

To my friends and family, I am thankful for the support throughout the journey from starting to think this could be an important topic to knowing it was. They listened and constructively offered opinions along the way and helped me to find the right words to bring this to life.

And years ago, one of my work colleagues challenged me on this topic. He asked, "Improv at work? I don't get it. Improv is about flying by the seat of your pants; we can't do that at work." Though now, I may call him a Lid, then it forced me to look more deeply as to what, why, and how. This look would lead me to where I am now: an absolute believer that we all *can* and *should* bring improv to work to create the workplace we all want and where we all can be happy and appreciated. So, thank you, cynical workplace friend, you only made me want to put this book out there more!

ABOUT THE AUTHOR

Nicole Faust Cohen is an experienced business leader and lifelong student and practitioner of the performing arts. She also has training and experience in both scripted performances, as well as the dynamic world of improvisational comedy.

Ms. Cohen is a managing director at a global consulting firm. Spending time with dozens of companies, she has seen both incredible collaborations, as well as those stifled by professionals who seemed to have forgotten that the journey towards greatness is as important as the greatness itself. Equally important, the journey may affect how great the outcomes can be.

Ms. Cohen was named a Luminary by the Healthcare Businesswomen's Association, which recognizes individuals who have made a significant impact on the healthcare industry, serve as a role model, actively mentor others, exhibit dedication to the industry, and consistently demonstrate exceptional leadership.

Outside her industry work, Ms. Cohen creates and leads workshops on the topic of bringing the rules of improvisational comedy to the workplace, for the purpose of creating the most collaborative and innovative work environment possible.

Ms. Cohen graduated from Northwestern University with a Bachelor of Science in Biomedical Engineering and a theme in Fine Arts/Theatre. It was in college where she became exposed to improvisational comedy, cast in an improv group called Titanic Players alongside a mighty cast of hilarious actors, who performed regularly.

Today, Ms. Cohen lives on the East Coast with her husband, kids, and their family dog.

www.ingramcontent.com/pod-product-compliance
Lightning Source LLC
Chambersburg PA
CBHW071417210326
41597CB00020B/3544